The Poetry Of Charles Kingsley

Charles Kingsley was born on June 12th 1819 in Holne Devon, a region of the Country for which he is now most associated.

He spent his early years in Devon and Northamptonshire before studying at King's College, London and Cambridge graduating from Magdalene College in 1843.

Wishing to pursue a career in the Church he was appointed Rector of Eversley in Hampshire in 1844.

In 1855 he published one of his two enduring novels; Westward Ho!

By 1859 he was chaplain to no less than Queen Victoria. By 1860 a Regius Professor at Cambridge and the following year he was the private tutor to the Prince Of Wales.

In 1853 The Water Babies was published and remains to this day a classic around the world.

Kingsley sat on the 1866 Edward Eyre Defence Committee along with Thomas Carlyle, John Ruskin, Charles Dickens and Alfred Lord Tennyson, where he supported Jamaican Governor Edward Eyre's brutal suppression of the Morant Bay Rebellion against the Jamaica Committee.

In 1869 Kingsley resigned his Cambridge professorship and, from 1870 to 1873, was a canon of Chester Cathedral.

In 1872 he accepted the Presidency of the Birmingham and Midland Institute and became its 19th President.

In 1873 he was made the canon of Westminster Abbey.

Charles Kingsley died in 1875 and was buried in St Mary's Churchyard in Eversley.

In this volume we publish his poetry which although partly neglected in the light of his above achievements is not to be dismissed. Many authors find a release in their poetry and for Kingsley amongst his novels and sermons are these undoubted gems.

Index Of Poems

A March
A Myth
A New Forest Ballad
A Parable From Liebig
A Thought From The Rhine
Airly Beacon
Alton Locke's Song
Andromeda
Ballad of Earl Haldan's Daughter
Ballad: Lorraine, Lorraine, Lorree
Child Ballad
Christmas Day
Dartside, 1849
Dolcino To Margaret
Down To The Mothers
Drifting Away: A Fragment
Eversley, 1867.
Easter Week
Elegiacs
Fishing Song: To J.A. Froude and Tom Hughes
Frank Leigh's Song: A.D. 1586
Hymn
Hypotheses Hypochondriacae
In An Illuminated Missal
Juventus Mundi
Lorraine
Margaret To Dolcino
Martin Lightfoot's Song
My Hunting Song
My Little Doll
Ode On The Istallation of the Duke of Devonshire
Ode to the Northeast Wind
Oh! That We Two Were Maying
Old And New: A Parable
On The Death of A Certain Journal
On The Death of Leopold: King of The Belgians
Palinodia
Pen-Y-Gwrydd: To Tom Hughes, Esq.,
Qu'est Qu'il Dit'
Saint Maura: A.D. 304
Sappho
Scotch Song
Sing Heigh-Ho!
Sonnet
The Bad Squire
The Day of The Lord
The Dead Church
The Delectable Day
The Find
The Invitation: To Tom Hughes
The Knight's Leap: A Legend of Altenar
The Knight's Return

1st September 1870
Speak low, speak little; who may sing
While yonder cannon-thunders boom?
Watch, shuddering, what each day may bring:
Nor 'pipe amid the crack of doom.'

And yet-the pines sing overhead,
The robins by the alder-pool,
The bees about the garden-bed,
The children dancing home from school.

And ever at the loom of Birth
The mighty Mother weaves and sings:
She weaves-fresh robes for mangled earth;
She sings-fresh hopes for desperate things.

And thou, too: if through Nature's calm
Some strain of music touch thine ears,

Accept and share that soothing balm,
And sing, though choked with pitying tears.

A Christmas Carol

It chanced upon the merry merry Christmas eve,
I went sighing past the church across the moorland dreary-
'Oh! never sin and want and woe this earth will leave,
And the bells but mock the wailing round, they sing so cheery.
How long, O Lord! how long before Thou come again?
Still in cellar, and in garret, and on moorland dreary
The orphans moan, and widows weep, and poor men toil in vain,
Till earth is sick of hope deferred, though Christmas bells be cheery.'

Then arose a joyous clamour from the wild-fowl on the mere,
Beneath the stars, across the snow, like clear bells ringing,
And a voice within cried-'Listen!-Christmas carols even here!
Though thou be dumb, yet o'er their work the stars and snows are singing.
Blind! I live, I love, I reign; and all the nations through
With the thunder of my judgments even now are ringing.
Do thou fulfil thy work but as yon wild-fowl do,
Thou wilt heed no less the wailing, yet hear through it angels singing.'

A Farewell

I
My fairest child, I have no song to give you;
No lark could pipe to skies so dull and grey:
Yet, ere we part, one lesson I can leave you
For every day.

II
Be good, sweet maid, and let who will be clever;
Do noble things, not dream them, all day long:
And so make life, death, and that vast for-ever
One grand, sweet song.

A Farewell: To C.E.G

My fairest child, I have no song to give you;
No lark could pipe in skies so dull and gray;
Yet, if you will, one quiet hint I'll leave you,
For every day.

I'll tell you how to sing a clearer carol
Than lark who hails the dawn or breezy down;
To earn yourself a purer poet's laurel
Than Shakespeare's crown.

Be good, sweet maid, and let who can be clever;
Do lovely things, not dream them, all day long;

And so make Life, and Death, and that For Ever,
One grand sweet song.

A Hope

Twin stars, aloft in ether clear,
Around each other roll alway,
Within one common atmosphere
Of their own mutual light and day.

And myriad happy eyes are bent
Upon their changeless love alway;
As, strengthened by their one intent,
They pour the flood of life and day.

So we through this world's waning night
May, hand in hand, pursue our way;
Shed round us order, love, and light,
And shine unto the perfect day.

A Lament

The merry merry lark was up and singing,
And the hare was out and feeding on the lea;
And the merry merry bells below were ringing,
When my child's laugh rang through me.

Now the hare is snared and dead beside the snow-yard,
And the lark beside the dreary winter sea;
And the baby in his cradle in the churchyard
Sleeps sound till the bell brings me.

A March

Dreary East winds howling o'er us;
Clay-lands knee-deep spread before us;
Mire and ice and snow and sleet;
Aching backs and frozen feet;
Knees which reel as marches quicken,
Ranks which thin as corpses thicken;
While with carrion birds we eat,
Calling puddle-water sweet,
As we pledge the health of our general, who fares as rough as we:
What can daunt us, what can turn us, led to death by such as he?

A Myth

A floating, a floating
Across the sleeping sea,
All night I heard a singing bird
Upon the topmast tree.

"Oh, came you from the isles of Greece
Or from the banks of Seine;
Or off some tree in forests free,
Which fringe the western main?"

"I came not off the old world
Nor yet from off the new—
But I am one of the birds of God
Which sing the whole night through."

"Oh, sing and wake the dawning—
Oh, whistle for the wind;
The night is long, the current strong,
My boat it lags behind."

"The current sweeps the old world,
The current sweeps the new;
The wind will blow, the dawn will glow,
Ere thou hast sail'd them through."

A New Forest Ballad
Oh she tripped over Ocknell plain,
And down by Bradley Water;
And the fairest maid on the forest side
Was Jane, the keeper's daughter.

She went and went through the broad gray lawns
As down the red sun sank,
And chill as the scent of a new-made grave
The mist smelt cold and dank.

'A token, a token!' that fair maid cried,
'A token that bodes me sorrow;
For they that smell the grave by night
Will see the corpse to-morrow.

'My own true love in Burley Walk
Does hunt to-night, I fear;
And if he meet my father stern,
His game may cost him dear.

'Ah, here's a curse on hare and grouse,
A curse on hart and hind;
And a health to the squire in all England,
Leaves never a head behind.'

Her true love shot a mighty hart
Among the standing rye,
When on him leapt that keeper old
From the fern where he did lie.

The forest laws were sharp and stern,
The forest blood was keen;
They lashed together for life and death
Beneath the hollies green.

The metal good and the walnut wood
Did soon in flinders flee;
They tost the orts to south and north,
And grappled knee to knee.

They wrestled up, they wrestled down,
They wrestled still and sore;
Beneath their feet the myrtle sweet
Was stamped to mud and gore.

Ah, cold pale moon, thou cruel pale moon,
That starest with never a frown
On all the grim and the ghastly things
That are wrought in thorpe and town:

And yet, cold pale moon, thou cruel pale moon,
That night hadst never the grace
To lighten two dying Christian men
To see one another's face.

They wrestled up, they wrestled down,
They wrestled sore and still,
The fiend who blinds the eyes of men
That night he had his will.

Like stags full spent, among the bent
They dropped a while to rest;
When the young man drove his saying knife
Deep in the old man's breast.

The old man drove his gunstock down
Upon the young man's head;
And side by side, by the water brown,
Those yeomen twain lay dead.

They dug three graves in Lyndhurst yard;
They dug them side by side;
Two yeomen lie there, and a maiden fair
A widow and never a bride.

A Parable From Liebig
The church bells were ringing, the devil sat singing
On the stump of a rotting old tree;
'Oh faith it grows cold, and the creeds they grow old,
And the world is nigh ready for me.'

The bells went on ringing, a spirit came singing,
And smiled as he crumbled the tree;
'Yon wood does but perish new seedlings to cherish,
And the world is too live yet for thee.'

A Thought From The Rhine
I heard an Eagle crying all alone
Above the vineyards through the summer night,
Among the skeletons of robber towers:
Because the ancient eyrie of his race
Was trenched and walled by busy-handed men;
And all his forest-chace and woodland wild,
Wherefrom he fed his young with hare and roe,
Were trim with grapes which swelled from hour to hour,
And tossed their golden tendrils to the sun
For joy at their own riches:-So, I thought,
The great devourers of the earth shall sit,
Idle and impotent, they know not why,
Down-staring from their barren height of state
On nations grown too wise to slay and slave,
The puppets of the few; while peaceful lore
And fellow-help make glad the heart of earth,
With wonders which they fear and hate, as he,
The Eagle, hates the vineyard slopes below.

Airly Beacon
Airly Beacon, Airly Beacon;
Oh, the pleasant sight to see
Shires and towns from Airly Beacon,
While my love climbed up to me!

Airly Beacon, Airly Beacon;
Oh, the happy hours we lay
Deep in fern on Airly Beacon,
Courting through the summer's day!

Airly Beacon, Airly Beacon;
Oh, the weary haunt for me,
All alone on Airly Beacon,
With his baby on my knee!

Alton Locke's Song
Weep, weep, weep and weep,
For pauper, dolt, and slave!
Hark! from wasted moor and fen,
Feverous alley, stifling den,
Swells the wail of Saxon men-
Work! or the grave!

Down, down, down and down,
With idler, knave, and tyrant!
Why for sluggards cark and moil?
He that will not live by toil
Has no right on English soil!
God's word's our warrant!

Up, up, up and up!
Face your game and play it!
The night is past, behold the sun!
The idols fall, the lie is done!
The Judge is set, the doom begun!
Who shall stay it?

Andromeda

Over the sea, past Crete, on the Syrian shore to the southward,
Dwells in the well-tilled lowland a dark-haired AEthiop people,
Skilful with needle and loom, and the arts of the dyer and carver,
Skilful, but feeble of heart; for they know not the lords of Olympus,
Lovers of men; neither broad-browed Zeus, nor Pallas Athene,
Teacher of wisdom to heroes, bestower of might in the battle;
Share not the cunning of Hermes, nor list to the songs of Apollo.
Fearing the stars of the sky, and the roll of the blue salt water,
Fearing all things that have life in the womb of the seas and the livers,
Eating no fish to this day, nor ploughing the main, like the Phoenics,
Manful with black-beaked ships, they abide in a sorrowful region,
Vexed with the earthquake, and flame, and the sea-floods, scourge of Poseidon.
Whelming the dwellings of men, and the toils of the slow-footed oxen,
Drowning the barley and flax, and the hard-earned gold of the harvest,
Up to the hillside vines, and the pastures skirting the woodland,
Inland the floods came yearly; and after the waters a monster,
Bred of the slime, like the worms which are bred from the slime of the Nile-bank,
Shapeless, a terror to see; and by night it swam out to the seaward,
Daily returning to feed with the dawn, and devoured of the fairest,
Cattle, and children, and maids, till the terrified people fled inland.
Fasting in sackcloth and ashes they came, both the king and his people,
Came to the mountain of oaks, to the house of the terrible sea-gods,
Hard by the gulf in the rocks, where of old the world-wide deluge
Sank to the inner abyss; and the lake where the fish of the goddess,
Holy, undying, abide; whom the priests feed daily with dainties.
There to the mystical fish, high-throned in her chamber of cedar,
Burnt they the fat of the flock; till the flame shone far to the seaward.
Three days fasting they prayed; but the fourth day the priests of the goddess,
Cunning in spells, cast lots, to discover the crime of the people.
All day long they cast, till the house of the monarch was taken,
Cepheus, king of the land; and the faces of all gathered blackness.
Then once more they cast; and Cassiopoeia was taken,

Deep-bosomed wife of the king, whom oft far-seeing Apollo
Watched well-pleased from the welkin, the fairest of AEthiop women:
Fairest, save only her daughter; for down to the ankle her tresses
Rolled, blue-black as the night, ambrosial, joy to beholders.
Awful and fair she arose, most like in her coming to Here,
Queen before whom the Immortals arise, as she comes on Olympus,
Out of the chamber of gold, which her son Hephaestos has wrought her.
Such in her stature and eyes, and the broad white light of her forehead.
Stately she came from her place, and she spoke in the midst of the people.
'Pure are my hands from blood: most pure this heart in my bosom.
Yet one fault I remember this day; one word have I spoken;
Rashly I spoke on the shore, and I dread lest the sea should have heard it.
Watching my child at her bath, as she plunged in the joy of her girlhood,
Fairer I called her in pride than Atergati, queen of the ocean.
Judge ye if this be my sin, for I know none other.' She ended;
Wrapping her head in her mantle she stood, and the people were silent.
Answered the dark-browed priests, 'No word, once spoken, returneth,
Even if uttered unwitting. Shall gods excuse our rashness?
That which is done, that abides; and the wrath of the sea is against us;
Hers, and the wrath of her brother, the Sun-god, lord of the sheepfolds.
Fairer than her hast thou boasted thy daughter? Ah folly! for hateful,
Hateful are they to the gods, whoso, impious, liken a mortal,
Fair though he be, to their glory; and hateful is that which is likened,
Grieving the eyes of their pride, and abominate, doomed to their anger.
What shall be likened to gods? The unknown, who deep in the darkness
Ever abide, twyformed, many-handed, terrible, shapeless.
Woe to the queen; for the land is defiled, and the people accursed.
Take thou her therefore by night, thou ill-starred Cassiopoeia,
Take her with us in the night, when the moon sinks low to the westward;
Bind her aloft for a victim, a prey for the gorge of the monster,
Far on the sea-girt rock, which is washed by the surges for ever;
So may the goddess accept her, and so may the land make atonement,
Purged by her blood from its sin: so obey thou the doom of the rulers.'
Bitter in soul they went out, Cepheus and Cassiopoeia,
Bitter in soul; and their hearts whirled round, as the leaves in the eddy.
Weak was the queen, and rebelled: but the king, like a shepherd of people,
Willed not the land should waste; so he yielded the life of his daughter.
Deep in the wane of the night, as the moon sank low to the westward,
They by the shade of the cliffs, with the horror of darkness around them,
Stole, as ashamed, to a deed which became not the light of the sunshine,
Slowly, the priests, and the queen, and the virgin bound in the galley,
Slowly they rowed to the rocks: but Cepheus far in the palace
Sate in the midst of the hall, on his throne, like a shepherd of people,
Choking his woe, dry-eyed, while the slaves wailed loudly around him.
They on the sea-girt rock, which is washed by the surges for ever,
Set her in silence, the guiltless, aloft with her face to the eastward.
Under a crag of the stone, where a ledge sloped down to the water;
There they set Andromeden, most beautiful, shaped like a goddess,
Lifting her long white arms wide-spread to the walls of the basalt,
Chaining them, ruthless, with brass; and they called on the might of the
Rulers.
'Mystical fish of the seas, dread Queen whom AEthiops honour,

Whelming the land in thy wrath, unavoidable, sharp as the sting-ray,
Thou, and thy brother the Sun, brain-smiting, lord of the sheepfold,
Scorching the earth all day, and then resting at night in thy bosom,
Take ye this one life for many, appeased by the blood of a maiden,
Fairest, and born of the fairest, a queen, most priceless of victims.'
Thrice they spat as they went by the maid: but her mother delaying
Fondled her child to the last, heart-crushed; and the warmth of her weeping
Fell on the breast of the maid, as her woe broke forth into wailing.
'Daughter! my daughter! forgive me! Oh curse not the murderess! Curse
not!
How have I sinned, but in love? Do the gods grudge glory to mothers?
Loving I bore thee in vain in the fate-cursed bride-bed of Cepheus,
Loving I fed thee and tended, and loving rejoiced in thy beauty,
Blessing thy limbs as I bathed them, and blessing thy locks as I combed them;
Decking thee, ripening to woman, I blest thee: yet blessing I slew thee!
How have I sinned, but in love? Oh swear to me, swear to thy mother,
Never to haunt me with curse, as I go to the grave in my sorrow,
Childless and lone: may the gods never send me another, to slay it!
See, I embrace thy knees-soft knees, where no babe will be fondled-
Swear to me never to curse me, the hapless one, not in the death-pang.'
Weeping she clung to the knees of the maid; and the maid low answered-
'Curse thee! Not in the death-pang!' The heart of the lady was lightened.
Slowly she went by the ledge; and the maid was alone in the darkness.
Watching the pulse of the oars die down, as her own died with them,
Tearless, dumb with amaze she stood, as a storm-stunned nestling
Fallen from bough or from eave lies dumb, which the home-going herdsman
Fancies a stone, till he catches the light of its terrified eyeball.
So through the long long hours the maid stood helpless and hopeless,
Wide-eyed, downward gazing in vain at the black blank darkness.
Feebly at last she began, while wild thoughts bubbled within her-
'Guiltless I am: why thus, then? Are gods more ruthless than mortals?
Have they no mercy for youth? no love for the souls who have loved them?
Even as I loved thee, dread sea, as I played by thy margin,
Blessing thy wave as it cooled me, thy wind as it breathed on my forehead,
Bowing my head to thy tempest, and opening my heart to thy children,
Silvery fish, wreathed shell, and the strange lithe things of the water,
Tenderly casting them back, as they gasped on the beach in the sunshine,
Home to their mother-in vain! for mine sits childless in anguish!
O false sea! false sea! I dreamed what I dreamed of thy goodness;
Dreamed of a smile in thy gleam, of a laugh in the plash of thy ripple:
False and devouring thou art, and the great world dark and despiteful.'
Awed by her own rash words she was still: and her eyes to the seaward
Looked for an answer of wrath: far off, in the heart of the darkness,
Blight white mists rose slowly; beneath them the wandering ocean
Glimmered and glowed to the deepest abyss; and the knees of the maiden
Trembled and sunk in her fear, as afar, like a dawn in the midnight,
Rose from their seaweed chamber the choir of the mystical sea-maids.
Onward toward her they came, and her heart beat loud at their coming,
Watching the bliss of the gods, as they wakened the cliffs with their
laughter.
Onward they came in their joy, and before them the roll of the surges
Sank, as the breeze sank dead, into smooth green foam-flecked marble,

Awed; and the crags of the cliff, and the pines of the mountain were silent.
Onward they came in their joy, and around them the lamps of the sea-nymphs,
Myriad fiery globes, swam panting and heaving; and rainbows
Crimson and azure and emerald, were broken in star-showers, lighting
Far through the wine-dark depths of the crystal, the gardens of Nereus,
Coral and sea-fan and tangle, the blooms and the palms of the ocean.
Onward they came in their joy, more white than the foam which they scattered,
Laughing and singing, and tossing and twining, while eager, the Tritons
Blinded with kisses their eyes, unreproved, and above them in worship
Hovered the terns, and the seagulls swept past them on silvery pinions
Echoing softly their laughter; around them the wantoning dolphins
Sighed as they plunged, full of love; and the great sea-horses which bore them
Curved up their crests in their pride to the delicate arms of the maidens,
Pawing the spray into gems, till a fiery rainfall, unharming,
Sparkled and gleamed on the limbs of the nymphs, and the coils of the mermen.
Onward they went in their joy, bathed round with the fiery coolness,
Needing nor sun nor moon, self-lighted, immortal: but others,
Pitiful, floated in silence apart; in their bosoms the sea-boys,
Slain by the wrath of the seas, swept down by the anger of Nereus;
Hapless, whom never again on strand or on quay shall their mothers
Welcome with garlands and vows to the temple, but wearily pining
Gaze over island and bay for the sails of the sunken; they heedless
Sleep in soft bosoms for ever, and dream of the surge and the sea-maids.
Onward they passed in their joy; on their brows neither sorrow nor anger;
Self-sufficing, as gods, never heeding the woe of the maiden.
She would have shrieked for their mercy: but shame made her dumb; and their eyeballs
Stared on her careless and still, like the eyes in the house of the idols.
Seeing they saw not, and passed, like a dream, on the murmuring ripple.
Stunned by the wonder she gazed, wide-eyed, as the glory departed.
'O fair shapes! far fairer than I! Too fair to be ruthless!
Gladden mine eyes once more with your splendour, unlike to my fancies;
You, then, smiled in the sea-gleam, and laughed in the plash of the ripple.
Awful I deemed you and formless; inhuman, monstrous as idols;
Lo, when ye came, ye were women, more loving and lovelier, only;
Like in all else; and I blest you: why blest ye not me for my worship?
Had you no mercy for me, thus guiltless? Ye pitied the sea-boys:
Why not me, then, more hapless by far? Does your sight and your knowledge
End with the marge of the waves? Is the world which ye dwell in not our world?'

Over the mountain aloft ran a rush and a roll and a roaring;
Downward the breeze came indignant, and leapt with a howl to the water,
Roaring in cranny and crag, till the pillars and clefts of the basalt
Rang like a god-swept lyre, and her brain grew mad with the noises;
Crashing and lapping of waters, and sighing and tossing of weed-beds,
Gurgle and whisper and hiss of the foam, while thundering surges
Boomed in the wave-worn halls, as they champed at the roots of the mountain.
Hour after hour in the darkness the wind rushed fierce to the landward,
Drenching the maiden with spray; she shivering, weary and drooping,

Stood with her heart full of thoughts, till the foam-crests gleamed in the twilight,
Leaping and laughing around, and the east grew red with the dawning.
Then on the ridge of the hills rose the broad bright sun in his glory,
Hurling his arrows abroad on the glittering crests of the surges,
Gilding the soft round bosoms of wood, and the downs of the coastland;
Gilding the weeds at her feet, and the foam-laced teeth of the ledges,
Showing the maiden her home through the veil of her locks, as they floated
Glistening, damp with the spray, in a long black cloud to the landward.
High in the far-off glens rose thin blue curls from the homesteads;
Softly the low of the herds, and the pipe of the outgoing herdsman,
Slid to her ear on the water, and melted her heart into weeping.
Shuddering, she tried to forget them; and straining her eyes to the seaward,
Watched for her doom, as she wailed, but in vain, to the terrible Sun-god.
'Dost thou not pity me, Sun, though thy wild dark sister be ruthless;
Dost thou not pity me here, as thou seest me desolate, weary,
Sickened with shame and despair, like a kid torn young from its mother?
What if my beauty insult thee, then blight it: but me-Oh spare me!
Spare me yet, ere he be here, fierce, tearing, unbearable! See me,
See me, how tender and soft, and thus helpless! See how I shudder,
Fancying only my doom. Wilt thou shine thus bright, when it takes me?
Are there no deaths save this, great Sun? No fiery arrow,
Lightning, or deep-mouthed wave? Why thus? What music in shrieking,
Pleasure in warm live limbs torn slowly? And dar'st thou behold them!
Oh, thou hast watched worse deeds! All sights are alike to thy brightness!
What if thou waken the birds to their song, dost thou waken no sorrow;
Waken no sick to their pain; no captive to wrench at his fetters?
Smile on the garden and fold, and on maidens who sing at the milking;
Flash into tapestried chambers, and peep in the eyelids of lovers,
Showing the blissful their bliss-Dost love, then, the place where thou smilest?
Lovest thou cities aflame, fierce blows, and the shrieks of the widow?
Lovest thou corpse-strewn fields, as thou lightest the path of the vulture?
Lovest thou these, that thou gazest so gay on my tears, and my mother's,
Laughing alike at the horror of one, and the bliss of another?
What dost thou care, in thy sky, for the joys and the sorrows of mortals?
Colder art thou than the nymphs: in thy broad bright eye is no seeing.
Hadst thou a soul-as much soul as the slaves in the house of my father,
Wouldst thou not save? Poor thralls! they pitied me, clung to me weeping,
Kissing my hands and my feet-What, are gods more ruthless than mortals?
Worse than the souls which they rule? Let me die: they war not with ashes!'
Sudden she ceased, with a shriek: in the spray, like a hovering foam-bow,
Hung, more fair than the foam-bow, a boy in the bloom of his manhood,
Golden-haired, ivory-limbed, ambrosial; over his shoulder
Hung for a veil of his beauty the gold-fringed folds of the goat-skin,
Bearing the brass of his shield, as the sun flashed clear on its clearness.
Curved on his thigh lay a falchion, and under the gleam of his helmet
Eyes more blue than the main shone awful; around him Athene
Shed in her love such grace, such state, and terrible daring.
Hovering over the water he came, upon glittering pinions,
Living, a wonder, outgrown from the tight-laced gold of his sandals;
Bounding from billow to billow, and sweeping the crests like a sea-gull;

Leaping the gulfs of the surge, as he laughed in the joy of his leaping.
Fair and majestic he sprang to the rock; and the maiden in wonder
Gazed for a while, and then hid in the dark-rolling wave of her tresses,
Fearful, the light of her eyes; while the boy (for her sorrow had awed him)
Blushed at her blushes, and vanished, like mist on the cliffs at the sunrise.
Fearful at length she looked forth: he was gone: she, wild with amazement,
Wailed for her mother aloud: but the wail of the wind only answered.
Sudden he flashed into sight, by her side; in his pity and anger
Moist were his eyes; and his breath like a rose-bed, as bolder and bolder,
Hovering under her brows, like a swallow that haunts by the house-eaves,
Delicate-handed, he lifted the veil of her hair; while the maiden
Motionless, frozen with fear, wept loud; till his lips unclosing
Poured from their pearl-strung portal the musical wave of his wonder.
'Ah, well spoke she, the wise one, the gray-eyed Pallas Athene,-
Known to Immortals alone are the prizes which lie for the heroes
Ready prepared at their feet; for requiring a little, the rulers
Pay back the loan tenfold to the man who, careless of pleasure,
Thirsting for honour and toil, fares forth on a perilous errand
Led by the guiding of gods, and strong in the strength of Immortals.
Thus have they led me to thee: from afar, unknowing, I marked thee,
Shining, a snow-white cross on the dark-green walls of the sea-cliff;
Carven in marble I deemed thee, a perfect work of the craftsman.
Likeness of Amphitrite, or far-famed Queen Cythereia.
Curious I came, till I saw how thy tresses streamed in the sea-wind,
Glistening, black as the night, and thy lips moved slow in thy wailing.
Speak again now-Oh speak! For my soul is stirred to avenge thee;
Tell me what barbarous horde, without law, unrighteous and heartless,
Hateful to gods and to men, thus have bound thee, a shame to the sunlight,
Scorn and prize to the sailor: but my prize now; for a coward,
Coward and shameless were he, who so finding a glorious jewel
Cast on the wayside by fools, would not win it and keep it and wear it,
Even as I will thee; for I swear by the head of my father,
Bearing thee over the sea-wave, to wed thee in Argos the fruitful,
Beautiful, meed of my toil no less than this head which I carry,
Hidden here fearful-Oh speak!'
But the maid, still dumb with amazement,
Watered her bosom with weeping, and longed for her home and her mother.
Beautiful, eager, he wooed her, and kissed off her tears as he hovered,
Roving at will, as a bee, on the brows of a rock nymph-haunted,
Garlanded over with vine, and acanthus, and clambering roses,
Cool in the fierce still noon, where streams glance clear in the mossbeds,
Hums on from blossom to blossom, and mingles the sweets as he tastes them.
Beautiful, eager, he kissed her, and clasped her yet closer and closer,
Praying her still to speak-
'Not cruel nor rough did my mother
Bear me to broad-browed Zeus in the depths of the brass-covered dungeon;
Neither in vain, as I think, have I talked with the cunning of Hermes,
Face unto face, as a friend; or from gray-eyed Pallas Athene
Learnt what is fit, and respecting myself, to respect in my dealings
Those whom the gods should love; so fear not; to chaste espousals
Only I woo thee, and swear, that a queen, and alone without rival
By me thou sittest in Argos of Hellas, throne of my fathers,

Worshipped by fair-haired kings: why callest thou still on thy mother?
Why did she leave thee thus here? For no foeman has bound thee; no foeman
Winning with strokes of the sword such a prize, would so leave it behind
him.'
Just as at first some colt, wild-eyed, with quivering nostril,
Plunges in fear of the curb, and the fluttering robes of the rider;
Soon, grown bold by despair, submits to the will of his master,
Tamer and tamer each hour, and at last, in the pride of obedience,
Answers the heel with a curvet, and arches his neck to be fondled,
Cowed by the need that maid grew tame; while the hero indignant
Tore at the fetters which held her: the brass, too cunningly tempered,
Held to the rock by the nails, deep wedged: till the boy, red with anger,
Drew from his ivory thigh, keen flashing, a falchion of diamond-
'Now let the work of the smith try strength with the arms of Immortals!'
Dazzling it fell; and the blade, as the vine-hook shears off the vine-bough,
Carved through the strength of the brass, till her arms fell soft on his
shoulder.
Once she essayed to escape: but the ring of the water was round her,
Round her the ring of his arms; and despairing she sank on his bosom.
Then, like a fawn when startled, she looked with a shriek to the seaward.
'Touch me not, wretch that I am! For accursed, a shame and a hissing,
Guiltless, accurst no less, I await the revenge of the sea-gods.
Yonder it comes! Ah go! Let me perish unseen, if I perish!
Spare me the shame of thine eyes, when merciless fangs must tear me
Piecemeal! Enough to endure by myself in the light of the sunshine
Guiltless, the death of a kid!'
But the boy still lingered around her,
Loth, like a boy, to forego her, and waken the cliffs with his laughter.
'Yon is the foe, then? A beast of the sea? I had deemed him immortal.
Titan, or Proteus' self, or Nereus, foeman of sailors:
Yet would I fight with them all, but Poseidon, shaker of mountains,
Uncle of mine, whom I fear, as is fit; for he haunts on Olympus,
Holding the third of the world; and the gods all rise at his coming.
Unto none else will I yield, god-helped: how then to a monster,
Child of the earth and of night, unreasoning, shapeless, accursed?'
'Art thou, too, then a god?'
'No god I,' smiling he answered;
'Mortal as thou, yet divine: but mortal the herds of the ocean,
Equal to men in that only, and less in all else; for they nourish
Blindly the life of the lips, untaught by the gods, without wisdom:
Shame if I fled before such!'
In her heart new life was enkindled,
Worship and trust, fair parents of love: but she answered him sighing.
'Beautiful, why wilt thou die? Is the light of the sun, then, so
worthless,
Worthless to sport with thy fellows in flowery glades of the forest,
Under the broad green oaks, where never again shall I wander,
Tossing the ball with my maidens, or wreathing the altar in garlands,
Careless, with dances and songs, till the glens rang loud to our laughter.
Too full of death the sad earth is already: the halls full of weepers,
Quarried by tombs all cliffs, and the bones gleam white on the sea-floor,
Numberless, gnawn by the herds who attend on the pitiless sea-gods,

Even as mine will be soon: and yet noble it seems to me, dying,
Giving my life for a people, to save to the arms of their lovers
Maidens and youths for a while: thee, fairest of all, shall I slay thee?
Add not thy bones to the many, thus angering idly the dread ones!
Either the monster will crush, or the sea-queen's self overwhelm thee,
Vengeful, in tempest and foam, and the thundering walls of the surges.
Why wilt thou follow me down? can we love in the black blank darkness?
Love in the realms of the dead, in the land where all is forgotten?
Why wilt thou follow me down? is it joy, on the desolate oozes,
Meagre to flit, gray ghosts in the depths of the gray salt water?
Beautiful! why wilt thou die, and defraud fair girls of thy manhood?
Surely one waits for thee longing, afar in the isles of the ocean.
Go thy way; I mine; for the gods grudge pleasure to mortals.'
Sobbing she ended her moan, as her neck, like a storm-bent lily,
Drooped with the weight of her woe, and her limbs sank, weary with watching,
Soft on the hard-ledged rock: but the boy, with his eye on the monster,
Clasped her, and stood, like a god; and his lips curved proud as he answered-
'Great are the pitiless sea-gods: but greater the Lords of Olympus;
Greater the AEgis-wielder, and greater is she who attends him.
Clear-eyed Justice her name is, the counsellor, loved of Athene;
Helper of heroes, who dare, in the god-given might of their manhood,
Greatly to do and to suffer, and far in the fens' and the forests
Smite the devourers of men, Heaven-hated, brood of the giants,
Twyformed, strange, without like, who obey not the golden-haired Rulers.
Vainly rebelling they rage, till they die by the swords of the heroes,
Even as this must die; for I burn with the wrath of my father,
Wandering, led by Athene; and dare whatsoever betides me.
Led by Athene I won from the gray-haired terrible sisters
Secrets hidden from men, when I found them asleep on the sand-hills,
Keeping their eye and their tooth, till they showed me the perilous pathway
Over the waterless ocean, the valley that led to the Gorgon.
Her too I slew in my craft, Medusa, the beautiful horror;
Taught by Athene I slew her, and saw not herself, but her image,
Watching the mirror of brass, in the shield which a goddess had lent me.
Cleaving her brass-scaled throat, as she lay with her adders around her,
Fearless I bore off her head, in the folds of the mystical goat-skin
Hide of Amaltheie, fair nurse of the AEgis-wielder.
Hither I bear it, a gift to the gods, and a death to my foe-men,
Freezing the seer to stone; to hide thine eyes from the horror.
Kiss me but once, and I go.'
Then lifting her neck, like a sea-bird
Peering up over the wave, from the foam-white swells of her bosom,
Blushing she kissed him: afar, on the topmost Idalian summit
Laughed in the joy of her heart, far-seeing, the queen Aphrodite.
Loosing his arms from her waist he flew upward, awaiting the sea-beast.
Onward it came from the southward, as bulky and black as a galley,
Lazily coasting along, as the fish fled leaping before it;
Lazily breasting the ripple, and watching by sandbar and headland,
Listening for laughter of maidens at bleaching, or song of the fisher,
Children at play on the pebbles, or cattle that pawed on the sand-hills.
Rolling and dripping it came, where bedded in glistening purple
Cold on the cold sea-weeds lay the long white sides of the maiden,

Trembling, her face in her hands, and her tresses afloat on the water.
As when an osprey aloft, dark-eyebrowed, royally crested,
Flags on by creek and by cove, and in scorn of the anger of Nereus
Ranges, the king of the shore; if he see on a glittering shallow,
Chasing the bass and the mullet, the fin of a wallowing dolphin,
Halting, he wheels round slowly, in doubt at the weight of his quarry,
Whether to clutch it alive, or to fall on the wretch like a plummet,
Stunning with terrible talon the life of the brain in the hindhead:
Then rushes up with a scream, and stooping the wrath of his eyebrows
Falls from the sky, like a star, while the wind rattles hoarse in his
pinions.
Over him closes the foam for a moment; and then from the sand-bed
Rolls up the great fish, dead, and his side gleams white in the sunshine.
Thus fell the boy on the beast, unveiling the face of the Gorgon;
Thus fell the boy on the beast; thus rolled up the beast in his horror,
Once, as the dead eyes glared into his; then his sides, death-sharpened,
Stiffened and stood, brown rock, in the wash of the wandering water.
Beautiful, eager, triumphant, he leapt back again to his treasure;
Leapt back again, full blest, toward arms spread wide to receive him.
Brimful of honour he clasped her, and brimful of love she caressed him,
Answering lip with lip; while above them the queen Aphrodite
Poured on their foreheads and limbs, unseen, ambrosial odours,
Givers of longing, and rapture, and chaste content in espousals.
Happy whom ere they be wedded anoints she, the Queen Aphrodite!
Laughing she called to her sister, the chaste Tritonid Athene,
'Seest thou yonder thy pupil, thou maid of the AEgis-wielder?
How he has turned himself wholly to love, and caresses a damsel,
Dreaming no longer of honour, or danger, or Pallas Athene?
Sweeter, it seems, to the young my gifts are; so yield me the stripling;
Yield him me now, lest he die in his prime, like hapless Adonis.'
Smiling she answered in turn, that chaste Tritonid Athene:
'Dear unto me, no less than to thee, is the wedlock of heroes;
Dear, who can worthily win him a wife not unworthy; and noble,
Pure with the pure to beget brave children, the like of their father.
Happy, who thus stands linked to the heroes who were, and who shall be;
Girdled with holiest awe, not sparing of self; for his mother
Watches his steps with the eyes of the gods; and his wife and his children
Move him to plan and to do in the farm and the camp and the council.
Thence comes weal to a nation: but woe upon woe, when the people
Mingle in love at their will, like the brutes, not heeding the future.'
Then from her gold-strung loom, where she wrought in her chamber of cedar,
Awful and fair she arose; and she went by the glens of Olympus;
Went by the isles of the sea, and the wind never ruffled her mantle;
Went by the water of Crete, and the black-beaked fleets of the Phoenics;
Came to the sea-girt rock which is washed by the surges for ever,
Bearing the wealth of the gods, for a gift to the bride of a hero.
There she met Andromeden and Persea, shaped like Immortals;
Solemn and sweet was her smile, while their hearts beat loud at her coming;
Solemn and sweet was her smile, as she spoke to the pair in her wisdom.
'Three things hold we, the Rulers, who sit by the founts of Olympus,
Wisdom, and prowess, and beauty; and freely we pour them on mortals;
Pleased at our image in man, as a father at his in his children.

One thing only we grudge to mankind: when a hero, unthankful,
Boasts of our gifts as his own, stiffnecked, and dishonours the givers,
Turning our weapons against us. Him Ate follows avenging;
Slowly she tracks him and sure, as a lyme-hound; sudden she grips him,
Crushing him, blind in his pride, for a sign and a terror to folly.
This we avenge, as is fit; in all else never weary of giving.
Come, then, damsel, and know if the gods grudge pleasure to mortals.'
Loving and gentle she spoke: but the maid stood in awe, as the goddess
Plaited with soft swift finger her tresses, and decked her in jewels,
Armlet and anklet and earbell; and over her shoulders a necklace,
Heavy, enamelled, the flower of the gold and the brass of the mountain.
Trembling with joy she gazed, so well Haephaistos had made it,
Deep in the forges of AEtna, while Charis his lady beside him
Mingled her grace in his craft, as he wrought for his sister Athene.
Then on the brows of the maiden a veil bound Pallas Athene;
Ample it fell to her feet, deep-fringed, a wonder of weaving.
Ages and ages agone it was wrought on the heights of Olympus,
Wrought in the gold-strung loom, by the finger of cunning Athene.
In it she wove all creatures that teem in the womb of the ocean;
Nereid, siren, and triton, and dolphin, and arrowy fishes
Glittering round, many-hued, on the flame-red folds of the mantle.
In it she wove, too, a town where gray-haired kings sat in judgment;
Sceptre in hand in the market they sat, doing right by the people,
Wise: while above watched Justice, and near, far-seeing Apollo.
Round it she wove for a fringe all herbs of the earth and the water,
Violet, asphodel, ivy, and vine-leaves, roses and lilies,
Coral and sea-fan and tangle, the blooms and the palms of the ocean:
Now from Olympus she bore it, a dower to the bride of a hero.
Over the limbs of the damsel she wrapt it: the maid still trembled,
Shading her face with her hands; for the eyes of the goddess were awful.
Then, as a pine upon Ida when southwest winds blow landward,
Stately she bent to the damsel, and breathed on her: under her breathing
Taller and fairer she grew; and the goddess spoke in her wisdom.
'Courage I give thee; the heart of a queen, and the mind of Immortals;
Godlike to talk with the gods, and to look on their eyes unshrinking;
Fearing the sun and the stars no more, and the blue salt water;
Fearing us only, the lords of Olympus, friends of the heroes;
Chastely and wisely to govern thyself and thy house and thy people,
Bearing a godlike race to thy spouse, till dying I set thee
High for a star in the heavens, a sign and a hope to the seamen,
Spreading thy long white arms all night in the heights of the aether,
Hard by thy sire and the hero thy spouse, while near thee thy mother
Sits in her ivory chair, as she plaits ambrosial tresses.
All night long thou wilt shine; all day thou wilt feast on Olympus,
Happy, the guest of the gods, by thy husband, the god-begotten.'
Blissful, they turned them to go: but the fair-tressed Pallas Athene
Rose, like a pillar of tall white cloud, toward silver Olympus;
Far above ocean and shore, and the peaks of the isles and the mainland;
Where no frost nor storm is, in clear blue windless abysses,
High in the home of the summer, the seats of the happy Immortals,
Shrouded in keen deep blaze, unapproachable; there ever youthful
Hebe, Harmonie, and the daughter of Jove, Aphrodite,

Whirled in the white-linked dance with the gold-crowned Hours and the Graces,
Hand within hand, while clear piped Phoebe, queen of the woodlands.
All day long they rejoiced: but Athene still in her chamber
Bent herself over her loom, as the stars rang loud to her singing,
Chanting of order and right, and of foresight, warden of nations;
Chanting of labour and craft, and of wealth in the port and the garner;
Chanting of valour and fame, and the man who can fall with the foremost,
Fighting for children and wife, and the field which his father bequeathed
him.
Sweetly and solemnly sang she, and planned new lessons for mortals:
Happy, who hearing obey her, the wise unsullied Athene.

Ballad of Earl Haldan's Daughter
It was Earl Haldan's daughter,
She looked across the sea;
She looked across the water;
And long and loud laughed she:
'The locks of six princesses
Must be my marriage fee,
So hey bonny boat, and ho bonny boat!
Who comes a wooing me?'

It was Earl Haldan's daughter,
She walked along the sand;
When she was aware of a knight so fair,
Came sailing to the land.
His sails were all of velvet,
His mast of beaten gold,
And 'Hey bonny boat, and ho bonny boat!
Who saileth here so bold?'

'The locks of five princesses
I won beyond the sea;
I clipt their golden tresses,
To fringe a cloak for thee.
One handful yet is wanting,
But one of all the tale;
So hey bonny boat, and ho bonny boat!
Furl up thy velvet sail!'

He leapt into the water,
That rover young and bold;
He gript Earl Haldan's daughter,
He clipt her locks of gold:
'Go weep, go weep, proud maiden,
The tale is full to-day.
Now hey bonny boat, and ho bonny boat!
Sail Westward ho! away!'

Ballad: Lorraine, Lorraine, Lorree

1

'Are you ready for your steeple-chase, Lorraine, Lorraine, Lorree?
Barum, Barum, Barum, Barum, Barum, Barum, Baree,
You're booked to ride your capping race to-day at Coulterlee,
You're booked to ride Vindictive, for all the world to see,
To keep him straight, to keep him first, and win the run for me.
Barum, Barum,' etc.

2

She clasped her new-born baby, poor Lorraine, Lorraine, Lorree,
'I cannot ride Vindictive, as any man might see,
And I will not ride Vindictive, with this baby on my knee;
He's killed a boy, he's killed a man, and why must he kill me?'

3

'Unless you ride Vindictive, Lorraine, Lorraine, Lorree,
Unless you ride Vindictive to-day at Coulterlee,
And land him safe across the brook, and win the blank for me,
It's you may keep your baby, for you'll get no keep from me.'

4

'That husbands could be cruel,' said Lorraine, Lorraine, Lorree,
'That husbands could be cruel, I have known for seasons three;
But oh! to ride Vindictive while a baby cries for me,
And be killed across a fence at last for all the world to see!'

5

She mastered young Vindictive-Oh! the gallant lass was she,
And kept him straight and won the race as near as near could be;
But he killed her at the brook against a pollard willow-tree,
Oh! he killed her at the brook, the brute, for all the world to see,
And no one but the baby cried for poor Lorraine, Lorree.

Child Ballad
Jesus, He loves one and all,
Jesus, He loves children small,
Their souls are waiting round His feet
On high, before His mercy-seat.

While He wandered here below
Children small to Him did go,
At His feet they knelt and prayed,
On their heads His hands He laid.

Came a Spirit on them then,
Better than of mighty men,
A Spirit faithful, pure and mild,
A Spirit fit for king and child.

Oh! that Spirit give to me,
Jesu Lord, where'er I be!

Christmas Day

How will it dawn, the coming Christmas Day?
A northern Christmas, such as painters love,
And kinsfolk, shaking hands but once a year,
And dames who tell old legends by the fire?
Red sun, blue sky, white snow, and pearled ice,
Keen ringing air, which sets the blood on fire,
And makes the old man merry with the young,
Through the short sunshine, through the longer night?
Or southern Christmas, dark and dank with mist,
And heavy with the scent of steaming leaves,
And rosebuds mouldering on the dripping porch;
One twilight, without rise or set of sun,
Till beetles drone along the hollow lane,
And round the leafless hawthorns, flitting bats
Hawk the pale moths of winter? Welcome then
At best, the flying gleam, the flying shower,
The rain-pools glittering on the long white roads,
And shadows sweeping on from down to down
Before the salt Atlantic gale: yet come
In whatsoever garb, or gay, or sad,
Come fair, come foul, 'twill still be Christmas Day.
How will it dawn, the coming Christmas Day?
To sailors lounging on the lonely deck
Beneath the rushing trade-wind? Or to him,
Who by some noisome harbour of the East,
Watches swart arms roll down the precious bales,
Spoils of the tropic forests; year by year
Amid the din of heathen voices, groaning
Himself half heathen? How to those-brave hearts!
Who toil with laden loins and sinking stride
Beside the bitter wells of treeless sands
Toward the peaks which flood the ancient Nile,
To free a tyrant's captives? How to those-
New patriarchs of the new-found underworld-
Who stand, like Jacob, on the virgin lawns,
And count their flocks' increase? To them that day
Shall dawn in glory, and solstitial blaze
Of full midsummer sun: to them that morn,
Gay flowers beneath their feet, gay birds aloft,
Shall tell of nought but summer: but to them,
Ere yet, unwarned by carol or by chime,
They spring into the saddle, thrills may come
From that great heart of Christendom which beats
Round all the worlds; and gracious thoughts of youth;
Of steadfast folk, who worship God at home;
Of wise words, learnt beside their mothers' knee;
Of innocent faces upturned once again
In awe and joy to listen to the tale
Of God made man, and in a manger laid-

May soften, purify, and raise the soul
From selfish cares, and growing lust of gain,
And phantoms of this dream which some call life,
Toward the eternal facts; for here or there,
Summer or winter, 'twill be Christmas Day.

Blest day, which aye reminds us, year by year,
What 'tis to be a man: to curb and spurn
The tyrant in us; that ignobler self
Which boasts, not loathes, its likeness to the brute,
And owns no good save ease, no ill save pain,
No purpose, save its share in that wild war
In which, through countless ages, living things
Compete in internecine greed.-Ah God!
Are we as creeping things, which have no Lord?
That we are brutes, great God, we know too well;
Apes daintier-featured; silly birds who flaunt
Their plumes unheeding of the fowler's step;
Spiders, who catch with paper, not with webs;
Tigers, who slay with cannon and sharp steel,
Instead of teeth and claws;-all these we are.
Are we no more than these, save in degree?
No more than these; and born but to compete-
To envy and devour, like beast or herb;
Mere fools of nature; puppets of strong lusts,
Taking the sword, to perish with the sword
Upon the universal battle-field,
Even as the things upon the moor outside?
The heath eats up green grass and delicate flowers,
The pine eats up the heath, the grub the pine,
The finch the grub, the hawk the silly finch;
And man, the mightiest of all beasts of prey,
Eats what he lists; the strong eat up the weak,
The many eat the few; great nations, small;
And he who cometh in the name of all-
He, greediest, triumphs by the greed of all;
And, armed by his own victims, eats up all:
While ever out of the eternal heavens
Looks patient down the great magnanimous God,
Who, Maker of all worlds, did sacrifice
All to Himself? Nay, but Himself to one;
Who taught mankind on that first Christmas Day,
What 'twas to be a man; to give, not take;
To serve, not rule; to nourish, not devour;
To help, not crush; if need, to die, not live.
O blessed day, which givest the eternal lie
To self, and sense, and all the brute within;
Oh, come to us, amid this war of life;
To hall and hovel, come; to all who toil
In senate, shop, or study; and to those
Who, sundered by the wastes of half a world,
Ill-warned, and sorely tempted, ever face

Nature's brute powers, and men unmanned to brutes-
Come to them, blest and blessing, Christmas Day.
Tell them once more the tale of Bethlehem;
The kneeling shepherds, and the Babe Divine:
And keep them men indeed, fair Christmas Day.

Dartside, 1849

I cannot tell what you say green leaves,
I cannot tell what you say:
But I know that there is a spirit in you,
And a word in you this day.

I cannot tell what you say, rosy rocks,
I cannot tell what you say:
But I know that there is a spirit in you,
And a word in you this day.

I cannot tell what you say, brown streams,
I cannot tell what you say:
But I know that in you too a spirit doth live,
And a word doth speak this day.

"Oh green is the colour of faith and truth,
And rose the colour of love and youth,
And brown of the fruitful clay.
Sweet Earth is faithful, and fruitful, and young,
And her bridal day shall come ere long,
And you shall know what the rocks and the streams
And the whispering woodlands say."

Dolcino To Margaret

The world goes up and the world goes down,
And the sunshine follows the rain;
And yesterday's sneer and yesterday's frown
Can never come over again,
Sweet wife:
No, never come over again.

For woman is warm though man be cold,
And the night will hallow the day;
Till the heart which at even was weary and old
Can rise in the morning gay,
Sweet wife;
To its work in the morning gay.

Down To The Mothers

Linger no more, my beloved, by abbey and cell and cathedral;
Mourn not for holy ones mourning of old them who knew not the Father,
Weeping with fast and scourge, when the bridegroom was taken from them.

Drop back awhile through the years, to the warm rich youth of the nations,
Childlike in virtue and faith, though childlike in passion and pleasure,
Childlike still, and still near to their God, while the day-spring of Eden
Lingered in rose-red rays on the peaks of Ionian mountains.
Down to the mothers, as Faust went, I go, to the roots of our manhood,
Mothers of us in our cradles; of us once more in our glory.
New-born, body and soul, in the great pure world which shall be
In the renewing of all things, when man shall return to his Eden
Conquering evil, and death, and shame, and the slander of conscience-
Free in the sunshine of Godhead-and fearlessly smile on his Father.
Down to the mothers I go-yet with thee still!-be with me, thou purest!
Lead me, thy hand in my hand; and the dayspring of God go before us.

Drifting Away: A Fragment
(Written for music to be sung at a parish industrial exhibition)

See the land, her Easter keeping,
Rises as her Maker rose.
Seeds, so long in darkness sleeping,
Burst at last from winter snows.
Earth with heaven above rejoices;
Fields and gardens hail the spring;
Shaughs and woodlands ring with voices,
While the wild birds build and sing.

You, to whom your Maker granted
Powers to those sweet birds unknown,
Use the craft by God implanted;
Use the reason not your own.
Here, while heaven and earth rejoices,
Each his Easter tribute bring-
Work of fingers, chant of voices,
Like the birds who build and sing.

Eversley, 1867.
They drift away. Ah, God! they drift for ever.
I watch the stream sweep onward to the sea,
Like some old battered buoy upon a roaring river,
Round whom the tide-waifs hang-then drift to sea.

I watch them drift-the old familiar faces,
Who fished and rode with me, by stream and wold,
Till ghosts, not men, fill old beloved places,
And, ah! the land is rank with churchyard mold.

I watch them drift-the youthful aspirations,
Shores, landmarks, beacons, drift alike.
. . . . .
I watch them drift-the poets and the statesmen;
The very streams run upward from the sea.

. . . . . .
Yet overhead the boundless arch of heaven
Still fades to night, still blazes into day.

. . . . .
Ah, God! My God! Thou wilt not drift away

Easter Week

See the land, her Easter keeping,
Rises as her Maker rose.
Seeds, so long in darkness sleeping,
Burst at last from winter snows.
Earth with heaven above rejoices;
Fields and gardens hail the spring;
Shaughs and woodlands ring with voices,
While the wild birds build and sing.

You, to whom your Maker granted
Powers to those sweet birds unknown,
Use the craft by God implanted;
Use the reason not your own.
Here, while heaven and earth rejoices,
Each his Easter tribute bring-
Work of fingers, chant of voices,
Like the birds who build and sing.

Elegiacs

Wearily stretches the sand to the surge, and the surge to the cloudland;
Wearily onward I ride, watching the water alone.
Not as of old, like Homeric Achilles,
Joyous knight-errant of God, thirsting for labour and strife;
No more on magical steed borne free through the regions of ether,
But, like the hack which I ride, selling my sinew for gold.
Fruit-bearing autumn is gone; let the sad quiet winter hang o'er me-
What were the spring to a soul laden with sorrow and shame?
Blossoms would fret me with beauty; my heart has no time to bepraise them;
Gray rock, bough, surge, cloud, waken no yearning within.
Sing not, thou sky-lark above! even angels pass hushed by the weeper.
Scream on, ye sea-fowl! my heart echoes your desolate cry.
Sweep the dry sand on, thou wild wind, to drift o'er the shell and the sea-weed;
Sea-weed and shell, like my dreams, swept down the pitiless tide.
Just is the wave which uptore us; 'tis Nature's own law which condemns us;
Woe to the weak who, in pride, build on the faith of the sand!
Joy to the oak of the mountain: he trusts to the might of the rock-clefts;
Deeply he mines, and in peace feeds on the wealth of the stone.

Fishing Song: To J.A. Froude and Tom Hughes

Oh, Mr. Froude, how wise and good,
To point us out this way to glory-

They're no great shakes, those Snowdon Lakes,
And all their pounders myth and story.
Blow Snowdon! What's Lake Gwynant to Killarney,
Or spluttering Welsh to tender blarney, blarney, blarney?

So Thomas Hughes, sir, if you choose,
I'll tell you where we think of going,
To swate and far o'er cliff and scar,
Hear horns of Elfland faintly blowing;
Blow Snowdon! There's a hundred lakes to try in,
And fresh caught salmon daily, frying, frying, frying.

Geology and botany
A hundred wonders shall diskiver,
We'll flog and troll in strid and hole,
And skim the cream of lake and river,
Blow Snowdon! give me Ireland for my pennies,
Hurrah! for salmon, grilse, and-Dennis, Dennis, Dennis!

Frank Leigh's Song: A.D. 1586
Ah tyrant Love, Megaera's serpents bearing,
Why thus requite my sighs with venom'd smart?
Ah ruthless dove, the vulture's talons wearing,
Why flesh them, traitress, in this faithful heart?
Is this my meed? Must dragons' teeth alone
In Venus' lawns by lovers' hands be sown?

Nay, gentlest Cupid; 'twas my pride undid me;
Nay, guiltless dove; by mine own wound I fell.
To worship, not to wed, Celestials bid me:
I dreamt to mate in heaven, and wake in hell;
For ever doom'd, Ixion-like, to reel
On mine own passions' ever-burning wheel.

Hymn
Accept this building, gracious Lord,
No temple though it be;
We raised it for our suffering kin,
And so, Good Lord, for Thee.

Accept our little gift, and give
To all who here may dwell,
The will and power to do their work,
Or bear their sorrows well.

From Thee all skill and science flow;
All pity, care, and love,
All calm and courage, faith and hope,
Oh! pour them from above.

And part them, Lord, to each and all,
As each and all shall need,
To rise like incense, each to Thee,
In noble thought and deed.

And hasten, Lord, that perfect day,
When pain and death shall cease;
And Thy just rule shall fill the earth
With health, and light, and peace.

When ever blue the sky shall gleam,
And ever green the sod;
And man's rude work deface no more
The Paradise of God.

Hypotheses Hypochondriacae

And should she die, her grave should be
Upon the bare top of a sunny hill,
Among the moorlands of her own fair land,
Amid a ring of old and moss-grown stones
In gorse and heather all embosomed.
There should be no tall stone, no marble tomb
Above her gentle corse;-the ponderous pile
Would press too rudely on those fairy limbs.
The turf should lightly he, that marked her home.
A sacred spot it would be-every bird
That came to watch her lone grave should be holy.
The deer should browse around her undisturbed;
The whin bird by, her lonely nest should build
All fearless; for in life she loved to see
Happiness in all things-
And we would come on summer days
When all around was bright, and set us down
And think of all that lay beneath that turf
On which the heedless moor-bird sits, and whistles
His long, shrill, painful song, as though he plained
For her that loved him and his pleasant hills;
And we would dream again of bygone days
Until our eyes should swell with natural tears
For brilliant hopes-all faded into air!
As, on the sands of Irak, near approach
Destroys the traveller's vision of still lakes,
And goodly streams reed-clad, and meadows green;
And leaves behind the drear reality
Of shadeless, same, yet ever-changing sand!
And when the sullen clouds rose thick on high
Mountains on mountains rolling-and dark mist
Wrapped itself round the hill-tops like a shroud,
When on her grave swept by the moaning wind
Bending the heather-bells-then would I come
And watch by her, in silent loneliness,

And smile upon the storm-as knowing well
The lightning's flash would surely turn aside,
Nor mar the lowly mound, where peaceful sleeps
All that gave life and love to one fond heart!
I talk of things that are not; and if prayers
By night and day availed from my weak lips,
Then should they never be! till I was gone,
Before the friends I loved, to my long home.
Oh pardon me, if e'er I say too much; my mind
Too often strangely turns to ribald mirth,
As though I had no doubt nor hope beyond-
Or brooding melancholy cloys my soul
With thoughts of days misspent, of wasted time
And bitter feelings swallowed up in jests.
Then strange and fearful thoughts flit o'er my brain
By indistinctness made more terrible,
And incubi mock at me with fierce eyes
Upon my couch: and visions, crude and dire,
Of planets, suns, millions of miles, infinity,
Space, time, thought, being, blank nonentity,
Things incorporeal, fancies of the brain,
Seen, heard, as though they were material,
All mixed in sickening mazes, trouble me,
And lead my soul away from earth and heaven
Until I doubt whether I be or not!
And then I see all frightful shapes-lank ghosts,
Hydras, chimeras, krakens, wastes of sand,
Herbless and void of living voice-tall mountains
Cleaving the skies with height immeasurable,
On which perchance I climb for infinite years; broad seas,
Studded with islands numberless, that stretch
Beyond the regions of the sun, and fade
Away in distance vast, or dreary clouds,
Cold, dark, and watery, where wander I for ever!
Or space of ether, where I hang for aye!
A speck, an atom-inconsumable-
Immortal, hopeless, voiceless, powerless!
And oft I fancy, I am weak and old,
And all who loved me, one by one, are dead,
And I am left alone-and cannot die!
Surely there is no rest on earth for souls
Whose dreams are like a madman's! I am young
And much is yet before me-after years
May bring peace with them to my weary heart!

In An Illuminated Missal
I would have loved: there are no mates in heaven;
I would be great: there is no pride in heaven;
I would have sung, as doth the nightingale
The summer's night beneath the moone pale,
But Saintes hymns alone in heaven prevail.

My love, my song, my skill, my high intent,
Have I within this seely book y-pent:
And all that beauty which from every part
I treasured still alway within mine heart,
Whether of form or face angelical,
Or herb or flower, or lofty cathedral,
Upon these sheets below doth lie y-spred,
In quaint devices deftly blazoned.
Lord, in this tome to thee I sanctify
The sinful fruits of worldly fantasy.

Juventus Mundi
List a tale a fairy sent us
Fresh from dear Mundi Juventus.
When Love and all the world was young,
And birds conversed as well as sung;
And men still faced this fair creation
With humour, heart, imagination.
Who come hither from Morocco
Every spring on the sirocco?
In russet she, and he in yellow,
Singing ever clear and mellow,
'Sweet, sweet, sweet, sweet, sweet you, sweet you,
Did he beat you? Did he beat you?'
Phyllopneustes wise folk call them,
But don't know what did befall them,
Why they ever thought of coming
All that way to hear gnats humming,
Why they built not nests but houses,
Like the bumble-bees and mousies.
Nor how little birds got wings,
Nor what 'tis the small cock sings-
How should they know-stupid fogies?
They daren't even believe in bogies.
Once they were a girl and boy,
Each the other's life and joy.
He a Daphnis, she a Chloe,
Only they were brown, not snowy,
Till an Arab found them playing
Far beyond the Atlas straying,
Tied the helpless things together,
Drove them in the burning weather,
In his slave-gang many a league,
Till they dropped from wild fatigue.
Up he caught his whip of hide,
Lashed each soft brown back and side
Till their little brains were burst
With sharp pain, and heat, and thirst,
Over her the poor boy lay,
Tried to keep the blows away,
Till they stiffened into clay,

And the ruffian rode away:
Swooping o'er the tainted ground,
Carrion vultures gathered round,
And the gaunt hyenas ran
Tracking up the caravan.
But-ah, wonder! that was gone
Which they meant to feast upon.
And, for each, a yellow wren,
One a cock, and one a hen,
Sweetly warbling, flitted forth
O'er the desert toward the north.
But a shade of bygone sorrow,
Like a dream upon the morrow,
Round his tiny brainlet clinging,
Sets the wee cock ever singing,
'Sweet, sweet, sweet, sweet, sweet you, sweet you,
Did he beat you? Did he beat you?'
Vultures croaked, and hopped, and flopped,
But their evening meal was stopped.
And the gaunt hyenas foul
Sat down on their tails to howl.
Northward towards the cool spring weather,
Those two wrens fled on together,
On to England o'er the sea,
Where all folks alike are free.
There they built a cabin, wattled
Like the huts where first they prattled,
Hatched and fed, as safe as may be,
Many a tiny feathered baby.
But in autumn south they go
Past the Straits and Atlas' snow,
Over desert, over mountain,
To the palms beside the fountain,
Where, when once they lived before, he
Told her first the old, old story.
'What do the doves say? Curuck Coo,
You love me and I love you.'

Lorraine

"Are you ready for your steeplechase, Lorraine, Lorraine, Lorree?
Barum, Barum, Barum, Barum, Barum, Barum, Baree.
You're booked to ride your capping race to-day at Coulterlee,
You're booked to ride Vindictive, for all the world to see,
To keep him straight, and keep him first, and win the run for me."
Barum, Barum, Barum, Barum, Barum, Barum, Baree.

She clasp'd her newborn baby, poor Lorraine, Lorraine, Lorrèe,
Barum, Barum, Barum, Barum, Barum, Barum, Baree.
"I cannot ride Vindictive, as any man might see,
And I will not ride Vindictive, with this baby on my knee;
He 's kill'd a boy, he 's kill'd a man, and why must he kill me?"

"Unless you ride Vindictive, Lorraine, Lorraine, Lorree,
Unless you ride Vindictive to-day at Coulterlee,
And land him safe across the brook, and win the blank for me,
It 's you may keep your baby, for you 'll get no keep from me."

"That husbands could be cruel," said Lorraine, Lorraine, Lorrèe,
"That husbands could be cruel, I have known for seasons three;
But oh, to ride Vindictive while a baby cries for me,
And be kill'd across a fence at last for all the world to see!"

She master'd young Vindictive—O, the gallant lass was she!
And kept him straight and won the race as near as near could be;
But he kill'd her at the brook against a pollard willow tree;
Oh! he kill'd her at the brook, the brute, for all the world to see,
And no one but the baby cried for poor Lorraine, Lorree.

Margaret To Dolcino

Ask if I love thee? Oh, smiles cannot tell
Plainer what tears are now showing too well.
Had I not loved thee, my sky had been clear:
Had I not loved thee, I had not been here,
Weeping by thee.

Ask if I love thee? How else could I borrow
Pride from man's slander, and strength from my sorrow?
Laugh when they sneer at the fanatic's bride,
Knowing no bliss, save to toil and abide
Weeping by thee.

Martin Lightfoot's Song

Come hearken, hearken, gentles all,
Come hearken unto me,
And I'll sing you a song of a Wood-Lyon
Came swimming out over the sea.

He ranged west, he ranged east,
And far and wide ranged he;
He took his bite out of every beast
Lives under the greenwood tree.

Then by there came a silly old wolf,
'And I'll serve you,' quoth he;
Quoth the Lyon, 'My paw is heavy enough,
So what wilt thou do for me?'

Then by there came a cunning old fox,
'And I'll serve you,' quoth he;
Quoth the Lyon, 'My wits are sharp enough
So what wilt thou do for me?'

Then by there came a white, white dove,
Flew off Our Lady's knee;
Sang 'It's I will be your true, true love,
If you'll be true to me.'

'And what will you do, you bonny white dove?
And what will you do for me?'
'Oh, it's I'll bring you to Our Lady's love,
In the ways of chivalrie.'

He followed the dove that Wood-Lyon
By mere and wood and wold,
Till he is come to a perfect knight,
Like the Paladin of old.

He ranged east, he ranged west,
And far and wide ranged he-
And ever the dove won him honour and fame
In the ways of chivalrie.

Then by there came a foul old sow,
Came rookling under the tree;
And 'It's I will be true love to you,
If you'll be true to me.'

'And what wilt thou do, thou foul old sow?
And what wilt thou do for me?'
'Oh, there hangs in my snout a jewel of gold,
And that will I give to thee.'

He took to the sow that Wood-Lyon;
To the rookling sow took he;
And the dove flew up to Our Lady's bosom;
And never again throve he.

My Hunting Song

Forward! Hark forward's the cry!
One more fence and we're out on the open,
So to us at once, if you want to live near us!
Hark to them, ride to them, beauties! as on they go,
Leaping and sweeping away in the vale below!
Cowards and bunglers, whose heart or whose eye is slow,
Find themselves staring alone.

So the great cause flashes by;
Nearer and clearer its purposes open,
While louder and prouder the world-echoes cheer us:
Gentlemen sportsmen, you ought to live up to us,
Lead us, and lift us, and hallo our game to us-
We cannot call the hounds off, and no shame to us-
Don't be left staring alone!

My Little Doll
I once had a sweet little doll, dears,
The prettiest doll in the world;
Her cheeks were so red and so white, dears,
And her hair was so charmingly curled.
But I lost my poor little doll, dears,
As I played in the heath one day;
And I cried for more than a week, dears,
But I never could find where she lay.

I found my poor little doll, dears,
As I played in the heath one day:
Folks say she is terribly changed, dears,
For her paint is all washed away,
And her arms trodden off by the cows, dears
And her hair not the least bit curled:
Yet for old sakes' sake she is still, dears,
The prettiest doll in the world.

Ode On The Istallation of the Duke of Devonshire
Hence a while, severer Muses;
Spare your slaves till drear October.
Hence; for Alma Mater chooses
Not to be for ever sober:
But, like stately matron gray,
Calling child and grandchild round her,
Will for them at least be gay;
Share for once their holiday;
And, knowing she will sleep the sounder,
Cheerier-hearted on the morrow
Rise to grapple care and sorrow,
Grandly leads the dance adown, and joins the children's play.
So go, for in your places
Already, as you see,
(Her tears for some deep sorrow scarcely dried),
Venus holds court among her sinless graces,
With many a nymph from many a park and lea.
She, pensive, waits the merrier faces
Of those your wittier sisters three,
O'er jest and dance and song who still preside,
To cheer her in this merry-mournful tide;
And bids us, as she smiles or sighs,
Tune our fancies by her eyes.

Then let the young be glad,
Fair girl and gallant lad,
And sun themselves to-day
By lawn and garden gay;
'Tis play befits the noon

Of rosy-girdled June:
Who dare frown if heaven shall smile?
Blest, who can forget a while;
The world before them, and above
The light of universal love.
Go, then, let the young be gay;
From their heart as from their dress
Let darkness and let mourning pass away,
While we the staid and worn look on and bless.

Health to courage firm and high!
Health to Granta's chivalry!
Wisely finding, day by day,
Play in toil, and toil in play.
Granta greets them, gliding down
On by park and spire and town;
Humming mills and golden meadows,
Barred with elm and poplar shadows;
Giant groves, and learned halls;
Holy fanes and pictured walls.
Yet she bides not here; around
Lies the Muses' sacred ground.
Most she lingers, where below
Gliding wherries come and go;
Stalwart footsteps shake the shores;
Rolls the pulse of stalwart oars;
Rings aloft the exultant cry
For the bloodless victory.
There she greets the sports, which breed
Valiant lads for England's need;
Wisely finding, day by day,
Play in toil, and toil in play.
Health to courage, firm and high!
Health to Granta's chivalry!

Yet stay a while, severer Muses, stay,
For you, too, have your rightful parts to-day.
Known long to you, and known through you to fame,
Are Chatsworth's halls, and Cavendish's name.
You too, then, Alma Mater calls to greet
A worthy patron for your ancient seat;
And bid her sons from him example take,
Of learning purely sought for learning's sake,
Of worth unboastful, power in duty spent;
And see, fulfilled in him, her high intent.

Come, Euterpe, wake thy choir;
Fit thy notes to our desire.
Long may he sit the chiefest here,
Meet us and greet us, year by year;
Long inherit, sire and son,
All that their race has wrought and won,

Since that great Cavendish came again,
Round the world and over the main,
Breasting the Thames with his mariners bold,
Past good Queen Bess's palace of old;
With jewel and ingot packed in his hold,
And sails of damask and cloth of gold;
While never a sailor-boy on board
But was decked as brave as a Spanish lord,
With the spoils he had won
In the Isles of the Sun,
And the shores of Fairy-land,
And yet held for the crown of the goodly show,
That queenly smile from the Palace window,
And that wave of a queenly hand.
Yes, let the young be gay,
And sun themselves to-day;-
And from their hearts, as from their dress,
Let mourning pass away.
But not from us, who watch our years fast fleeing,
And snatching as they flee, fresh fragments of our being.
Can we forget one friend,
Can we forget one face,
Which cheered us toward our end,
Which nerved us for our race?
Oh sad to toil, and yet forego
One presence which has made us know
To Godlike souls how deep our debt!
We would not, if we could, forget.

Severer Muses, linger yet;
Speak out for us one pure and rich regret.
Thou, Clio, who, with awful pen,
Gravest great names upon the hearts of men,
Speak of a fate beyond our ken;
A gem late found and lost too soon;
A sun gone down at highest noon;
A tree from Odin's ancient root,
Which bore for men the ancient fruit,
Counsel, and faith and scorn of wrong,
And cunning lore, and soothing song,
Snapt in mid-growth, and leaving unaware
The flock unsheltered and the pasture bare
Nay, let us take what God shall send,
Trusting bounty without end.
God ever lives; and Nature,
Beneath His high dictature,
Hale and teeming, can replace
Strength by strength, and grace by grace,
Hope by hope, and friend by friend:
Trust; and take what God shall send.
So shall Alma Mater see
Daughters fair and wise

Train new lands of liberty
Under stranger skies;
Spreading round the teeming earth
English science, manhood, worth.

Ode to the Northeast Wind

Welcome, wild Northeaster!
Shame it is to see
Odes to every zephyr;
Ne'er a verse to thee.
Welcome, black Northeaster!
O'er the German foam;
O'er the Danish moorlands,
From thy frozen home.
Tired are we of summer,
Tired of gaudy glare,
Showers soft and steaming,
Hot and breathless air.
Tired of listless dreaming,
Through the lazy day
Jovial wind of winter
Turn us out to play!
Sweep the golden reed-beds;
Crisp the lazy dike;
Hunger into madness
Every plunging pike.
Fill the lake with wild fowl;
Fill the marsh with snipe;
While on dreary moorlands
Lonely curlew pipe.
Through the black fir-forest
Thunder harsh and dry,
Shattering down the snowflakes
Off the curdled sky.
Hark! The brave Northeaster!
Breast-high lies the scent,
On by holt and headland,
Over heath and bent.
Chime, ye dappled darlings,
Through the sleet and snow.
Who can override you?
Let the horses go!
Chime, ye dappled darlings,
Down the roaring blast;
You shall see a fox die
Ere an hour be past.
Go! and rest tomorrow,
Hunting in your dreams,
While our skates are ringing
O'er the frozen streams.
Let the luscious Southwind

Breathe in lovers' sighs,
While the lazy gallants
Bask in ladies' eyes.
What does he but soften
Heart alike and pen?
'Tis the hard gray weather
Breeds hard English men.
What's the soft Southwester?
'Tis the ladies' breeze,
Bringing home their trueloves
Out of all the seas.
But the black Northeaster,
Through the snowstorm hurled,
Drives our English hearts of oak
Seaward round the world.
Come, as came our fathers,
Heralded by thee,
Conquering from the eastward,
Lords by land and sea.
Come; and strong, within us
Stir the Vikings' blood;
Bracing brain and sinew;
Blow, thou wind of God!

Oh! That We Two Were Maying
Oh! that we two were Maying
Down the stream of the soft spring breeze;
Like children with violets playing
In the shade of the whispering trees.

Oh! that we two sat dreaming
On the sward of some sheep-trimmed down,
Watching the white mist steaming
Over river and mead and town.

Oh! that we two lay sleeping
In our nest in the churchyard sod,
With our limbs at rest on the quiet earth's breast,
And our souls at home with God!

Old And New: A Parable
See how the autumn leaves float by decaying,
Down the wild swirls of the rain-swollen stream.
So fleet the works of men, back to their earth again;
Ancient and holy things fade like a dream.

Nay! see the spring-blossoms steal forth a-maying,
Clothing with tender hues orchard and glen;
So, though old forms pass by, ne'er shall their spirit die,
Look! England's bare boughs show green leaf again.

On The Death of A Certain Journal

So die, thou child of stormy dawn,
Thou winter flower, forlorn of nurse;
Chilled early by the bigot's curse,
The pedant's frown, the worldling's yawn.

Fair death, to fall in teeming June,
When every seed which drops to earth
Takes root, and wins a second birth
From steaming shower and gleaming moon.

Fall warm, fall fast, thou mellow rain;
Thou rain of God, make fat the land;
That roots which parch in burning sand
May bud to flower and fruit again.

To grace, perchance, a fairer morn
In mightier lands beyond the sea,
While honour falls to such as we
From hearts of heroes yet unborn,

Who in the light of fuller day,
Of purer science, holier laws,
Bless us, faint heralds of their cause,
Dim beacons of their glorious way.

Failure? While tide-floods rise and boil
Round cape and isle, in port and cove,
Resistless, star-led from above:
What though our tiny wave recoil?

On The Death of Leopold: King of The Belgians

A King is dead! Another master mind
Is summoned from the world-wide council hall.
Ah, for some seer, to say what links behind-
To read the mystic writing on the wall!

Be still, fond man: nor ask thy fate to know.
Face bravely what each God-sent moment brings.
Above thee rules in love, through weal and woe,
Guiding thy kings and thee, the King of kings.

Palinodia

Ye mountains, on whose torrent-furrowed slopes,
And bare and silent brows uplift to heaven,
I envied oft the soul which fills your wastes
Of pure and stern sublime, and still expanse
Unbroken by the petty incidents

Of noisy life: Oh hear me once again!

Winds, upon whose racked eddies, far aloft,
Above the murmur of the uneasy world,
My thoughts in exultation held their way:
Whose tremulous whispers through the rustling glade
Were once to me unearthly tones of love,
Joy without object, wordless music, stealing
Through all my soul, until my pulse beat fast
With aimless hope, and unexpressed desire-
Thou sea, who wast to me a prophet deep
Through all thy restless waves, and wasting shores,
Of silent labour, and eternal change;
First teacher of the dense immensity
Of ever-stirring life, in thy strange forms
Of fish, and shell, and worm, and oozy weed:
To me alike thy frenzy and thy sleep
Have been a deep and breathless joy: Oh hear!

Mountains, and winds, and waves, take back your child!
Upon thy balmy bosom, Mother Nature,
Where my young spirit dreamt its years away,
Give me once more to nestle: I have strayed
Far through another world, which is not thine.
Through sunless cities, and the weary haunts
Of smoke-grimed labour, and foul revelry
My flagging wing has swept. A mateless bird's
My pilgrimage has been; through sin, and doubt,
And darkness, seeking love. Oh hear me, Nature!
Receive me once again: but not alone;
No more alone, Great Mother! I have brought
One who has wandered, yet not sinned, like me.
Upon thy lap, twin children, let us lie;
And in the light of thine immortal eyes
Let our souls mingle, till The Father calls
To some eternal home the charge He gives thee.

Pen-Y-Gwrydd: To Tom Hughes, Esq.,
There is no inn in Snowdon which is not awful dear,
Excepting Pen-y-gwrydd (you can't pronounce it, dear),
Which standeth in the meeting of noble valleys three-
One is the vale of Gwynant, so well beloved by me,
One goes to Capel-Curig, and I can't mind its name,
And one it is Llanberris Pass, which all men knows the same;
Between which radiations vast mountains does arise,
As full of tarns as sieves of holes, in which big fish will rise,
That is, just one day in the year, if you be there, my boy,
Just about ten o'clock at night; and then I wish you joy.
Now to this Pen-y-gwrydd inn I purposeth to write,
(Axing the post town out of Froude, for I can't mind it quite),
And to engage a room or two, for let us say a week,

For fear of gents, and Manichees, and reading parties meek,
And there to live like fighting-cocks at almost a bob a day,
And arterwards toward the sea make tracks and cut away,
All for to catch the salmon bold in Aberglaslyn pool,
And work the flats in Traeth-Mawr, and will, or I'm a fool.
And that's my game, which if you like, respond to me by post;
But I fear it will not last, my son, a thirteen days at most.
Flies is no object; I can tell some three or four will do,
And John Jones, Clerk, he knows the rest, and ties and sells 'em too.
Besides of which I have no more to say, leastwise just now,
And so, goes to my children's school and 'umbly makes my bow.

Qu'est Qu'il Dit'

Espion aile de la jeune amante
De l'ombre des palmiers pourquoi ce cri?
Laisse en paix le beau garcon plaider et vaincre-
Pourquoi, pourquoi demander 'Qu'est qu'il dit?'

'Qu'est qu'il dit?' Ce que tu dis toi-meme
Chaque mois de ce printemps eternel;
Ce que disent les papillons qui s'entre-baisent,
Ce que dit tout bel jeun etre a toute belle.

Importun! Attende quelques lustres:
Quand les souvenirs 1'emmeneront ici-
Mere, grand'mere, pale, lasse, et fidele,
Demande mais doucement-'Et le vieillard,
Qu'est qu'il dit?'

Saint Maura: A.D. 304

Thank God! Those gazers' eyes are gone at last!
The guards are crouching underneath the rock;
The lights are fading in the town below,
Around the cottage which this morn was ours.
Kind sun, to set, and leave us here alone;
Alone upon our crosses with our God;
While all the angels watch us from the stars.
Kind moon, to shine so clear and full on him,
And bathe his limbs in glory, for a sign
Of what awaits him! Oh look on him, Lord!
Look, and remember how he saved thy lamb!
Oh listen to me, teacher, husband, love,
Never till now loved utterly! Oh say,
Say you forgive me! No-you must not speak:
You said it to me hours ago-long hours!
Now you must rest, and when to-morrow comes
Speak to the people, call them home to God,
A deacon on the Cross, as in the Church;
And plead from off the tree with outspread arms,

To show them that the Son of God endured
For them-and me. Hush! I alone will speak,
And while away the hours till dawn for you.
I know you have forgiven me; as I lay
Beneath your feet, while they were binding me,
I knew I was forgiven then! When I cried
'Here am I, husband! The lost lamb returned,
All re-baptized in blood!' and you said, 'Come!
Come to thy bride-bed, martyr, wife once more!'
From that same moment all my pain was gone;
And ever since those sightless eyes have smiled
Love-love! Alas, those eyes! They made me fall.
I could not bear to see them, bleeding, dark,
Never, no never to look into mine;
Never to watch me round the little room
Singing about my work, or flash on me
Looks bright with counsel.-Then they drove me mad
With talk of nameless tortures waiting you-
And I could save you! You would hear your love-
They knew you loved me, cruel men! And then-
Then came a dream; to say one little word,
One easy wicked word, we both might say,
And no one hear us, but the lictors round;
One tiny sprinkle of the incense grains,
And both, both free! And life had just begun-
Only three months-short months-your wedded wife
Only three months within the cottage there-
Hoping I bore your child. . . .
Ah! husband! Saviour! God! think gently of me!
I am forgiven! . . .
And then another dream;
A flash-so quick, I could not bear the blaze;
I could not see the smoke among the light-
To wander out through unknown lands, and lead
You by the hand through hamlet, port, and town,
On, on, until we died; and stand each day
To glory in you, as you preached and prayed
From rock and bourne-stone, with that voice, those words,
Mingled with fire and honey-you would wake,
Bend, save whole nations! would not that atone
For one short word?-ay, make it right, to save
You, you, to fight the battles of the Lord?
And so-and so-alas! you knew the rest!
You answered me. . . .
Ah cruel words! No! Blessed, godlike words.
You had done nobly had you struck me dead,
Instead of striking me to life!-the temptress! . . .
'Traitress! apostate! dead to God and me!'-
'The smell of death upon me?'-so it was!
True! true! well spoken, hero! Oh they snapped,
Those words, my madness, like the angel's voice
Thrilling the graves to birth-pangs. All was clear.

There was but one right thing in the world to do;
And I must do it. . . . Lord, have mercy! Christ!
Help through my womanhood: or I shall fail
Yet, as I failed before! . . . I could not speak-
I could not speak for shame and misery,
And terror of my sin, and of the things
I knew were coming: but in heaven, in heaven!
There we should meet, perhaps-and by that time
I might be worthy of you once again-
Of you, and of my God. . . . So I went out.
. . . . . .
Will you hear more, and so forget the pain?
And yet I dread to tell you what comes next;
Your love will feel it all again for me.
No! it is over; and the woe that's dead
Rises next hour a glorious angel. Love!
Say, shall I tell you? Ah! your lips are dry!
To-morrow, when they come, we must entreat,
And they will give you water. One to-day,
A soldier, gave me water in a sponge
Upon a reed, and said, 'Too fair! too young!
She might have been a gallant soldier's wife!'
And then I cried, 'I am a soldier's wife!
A hero's!' And he smiled, but let me drink.
God bless him for it!
So they led me back:
And as I went, a voice was in my ears
Which rang through all the sunlight, and the breath
And blaze of all the garden slopes below,
And through the harvest-voices, and the moan
Of cedar-forests on the cliffs above,
And round the shining rivers, and the peaks
Which hung beyond the cloud-bed of the west,
And round the ancient stones about my feet.
Out of all heaven and earth it rang, and cried,
'My hand hath made all these. Am I too weak
To give thee strength to say so?' Then my soul
Spread like a clear blue sky within my breast,
While all the people made a ring around,
And in the midst the judge spoke smilingly-
'Well! hast thou brought him to a better mind?'
'No! He has brought me to a better mind!'-
I cried, and said beside-I know not what-
Words which I learnt from thee-I trust in God
Nought fierce or rude-for was I not a girl
Three months ago beneath my mother's roof?
I thought of that. She might be there! I looked-
She was not there! I hid my face and wept.
And when I looked again, the judge's eye
Was on me, cold and steady, deep in thought-
'She knows what shame is still; so strip her.' 'Ah!'
I shrieked, 'Not that, Sir! Any pain! So young

I am-a wife too-I am not my own,
But his-my husband's!' But they took my shawl,
And tore my tunic off, and there I stood
Before them all. . . . Husband! you love me still?
Indeed I pleaded! Oh, shine out, kind moon,
And let me see him smile! Oh! how I prayed,
While some cried 'Shame!' and some, 'She is too young!'
And some mocked-ugly words: God shut my ears.
And yet no earthquake came to swallow me.
While all the court around, and walls, and roofs,
And all the earth and air were full of eyes,
Eyes, eyes, which scorched my limbs like burning flame,
Until my brain seemed bursting from my brow:
And yet no earthquake came! And then I knew
This body was not yours alone, but God's-
His loan-He needed it: and after that
The worst was come, and any torture more
A change-a lightening; and I did not shriek-
Once only-once, when first I felt the whip-
It coiled so keen around my side, and sent
A fire-flash through my heart which choked me-then
I shrieked-that once. The foolish echo rang
So far and long-I prayed you might not hear.
And then a mist, which hid the ring of eyes,
Swam by me, and a murmur in my ears
Of humming bees around the limes at home;
And I was all alone with you and God.
And what they did to me I hardly know;
I felt, and did not feel. Now I look back,
It was not after all so very sharp:
So do not pity me. It made me pray;
Forget my shame in pain, and pain in you,
And you in God: and once, when I looked down,
And saw an ugly sight-so many wounds!
'What matter?' thought I. 'His dear eyes are dark;
For them alone I kept these limbs so white-
A foolish pride! As God wills now. 'Tis just.'
But then the judge spoke out in haste: 'She is mad,
Or fenced by magic arts! She feels no pain!'
He did not know I was on fire within:
Better he should not; so his sin was less.
Then he cried fiercely, 'Take the slave away,
And crucify her by her husband's side!'
And at those words a film came on my face-
A sickening rush of joy-was that the end?
That my reward? I rose, and tried to go-
But all the eyes had vanished, and the judge;
And all the buildings melted into mist:
So how they brought me here I cannot tell-
Here, here, by you, until the judgment-day,
And after that for ever and for ever!
Ah! If I could but reach that hand! One touch!

One finger tip, to send the thrill through me
I felt but yesterday!-No! I can wait:-
Another body!-Oh, new limbs are ready,
Free, pure, instinct with soul through every nerve,
Kept for us in the treasuries of God.
They will not mar the love they try to speak,
They will not fail my soul, as these have done!
. . . . .
Will you hear more? Nay-you know all the rest:
Yet those poor eyes-alas! they could not see
My waking, when you hung above me there
With hands outstretched to bless the penitent-
Your penitent-even like The Lord Himself-
I gloried in you!-like The Lord Himself!
Sharing His very sufferings, to the crown
Of thorns which they had put on that dear brow
To make you like Him-show you as you were!
I told them so! I bid them look on you,
And see there what was the highest throne on earth-
The throne of suffering, where the Son of God
Endured and triumphed for them. But they laughed;
All but one soldier, gray, with many scars;
And he stood silent. Then I crawled to you,
And kissed your bleeding feet, and called aloud-
You heard me! You know all! I am at peace.
Peace, peace, as still and bright as is the moon
Upon your limbs, came on me at your smile,
And kept me happy, when they dragged me back
From that last kiss, and spread me on the cross,
And bound my wrists and ankles-Do not sigh:
I prayed, and bore it: and since they raised me up
My eyes have never left your face, my own, my own,
Nor will, till death comes! . . .
Do I feel much pain?
Not much. Not maddening. None I cannot bear.
It has become like part of my own life,
Or part of God's life in me-honour-bliss!
I dreaded madness, and instead comes rest;
Rest deep and smiling, like a summer's night.
I should be easy, now, if I could move . . .
I cannot stir. Ah God! these shoots of fire
Through all my limbs! Hush, selfish girl! He hears you!
Who ever found the cross a pleasant bed?
Yes; I can bear it, love. Pain is no evil
Unless it conquers us. These little wrists, now-
You said, one blessed night, they were too slender,
Too soft and slender for a deacon's wife-
Perhaps a martyr's:-You forgot the strength
Which God can give. The cord has cut them through;
And yet my voice has never faltered yet.
Oh! do not groan, or I shall long and pray
That you may die: and you must not die yet.

Not yet-they told us we might live three days . . .
Two days for you to preach! Two days to speak
Words which may wake the dead!
. . . . .
Hush! is he sleeping?
They say that men have slept upon the cross;
So why not he? . . . Thanks, Lord! I hear him breathe:
And he will preach Thy word to-morrow!-save
Souls, crowds, for Thee! And they will know his worth
Years hence-poor things, they know not what they do!-
And crown him martyr; and his name will ring
Through all the shores of earth, and all the stars
Whose eyes are sparkling through their tears to see
His triumph-Preacher! Martyr!-Ah-and me?-
If they must couple my poor name with his,
Let them tell all the truth-say how I loved him,
And tried to damn him by that love! O Lord!
Returning good for evil! and was this
The payment I deserved for such a sin?
To hang here on my cross, and look at him
Until we kneel before Thy throne in heaven!

Sappho
She lay among the myrtles on the cliff;
Above her glared the noon; beneath, the sea.
Upon the white horizon Atho's peak
Weltered in burning haze; all airs were dead;
The cicale slept among the tamarisk's hair;
The birds sat dumb and drooping. Far below
The lazy sea-weed glistened in the sun;
The lazy sea-fowl dried their steaming wings;
The lazy swell crept whispering up the ledge,
And sank again. Great Pan was laid to rest;
And Mother Earth watched by him as he slept,
And hushed her myriad children for a while.
She lay among the myrtles on the cliff;
And sighed for sleep, for sleep that would not hear,
But left her tossing still; for night and day
A mighty hunger yearned within her heart,
Till all her veins ran fever; and her cheek,
Her long thin hands, and ivory-channelled feet,
Were wasted with the wasting of her soul.
Then peevishly she flung her on her face,
And hid her eyeballs from the blinding glare,
And fingered at the grass, and tried to cool
Her crisp hot lips against the crisp hot sward:
And then she raised her head, and upward cast
Wild looks from homeless eyes, whose liquid light
Gleamed out between deep folds of blue-black hair,
As gleam twin lakes between the purple peaks
Of deep Parnassus, at the mournful moon.

Beside her lay her lyre. She snatched the shell,
And waked wild music from its silver strings;
Then tossed it sadly by.-'Ah, hush!' she cries;
'Dead offspring of the tortoise and the mine!
Why mock my discords with thine harmonies?
Although a thrice-Olympian lot be thine,
Only to echo back in every tone
The moods of nobler natures than thine own.'

Scotch Song

Oh, forth she went like a braw, braw bride
To meet her winsome groom,
When she was aware of twa bonny birds
Sat biggin' in the broom.

The tane it built with the green, green moss,
But and the bents sae fine,
And the tither wi' a lock o' lady's hair
Linked up wi' siller twine.

'O whaur gat ye the green, green moss,
O whaur the bents sae fine?
And whaur gat ye the bonny broun hair
That ance was tress o' mine?'

'We gat the moss fra' the elditch aile,
The bents fra' the whinny muir,
And a fause knight threw us the bonny broun hair,
To please his braw new fere.'

'Gae pull, gae pull the simmer leaves,
And strew them saft o'er me;
My token's tint, my love is fause,
I'll lay me doon and dee.'

Sing Heigh-Ho!

There sits a bird on every tree;
Sing heigh-ho!
There sits a bird on every tree,
And courts his love as I do thee;
Sing heigh-ho, and heigh-ho!
Young maids must marry.

There grows a flower on every bough;
Sing heigh-ho!
There grows a flower on every bough,
Its petals kiss-I'll show you how:
Sing heigh-ho, and heigh-ho!
Young maids must marry.

From sea to stream the salmon roam;
Sing heigh-ho!
From sea to stream the salmon roam;
Each finds a mate, and leads her home;
Sing heigh-ho, and heigh-ho!
Young maids must marry.

The sun's a bridegroom, earth a bride;
Sing heigh-ho!
They court from morn till eventide:
The earth shall pass, but love abide.
Sing heigh-ho, and heigh-ho!
Young maids must marry.

Sonnet

Oh, thou hadst been a wife for Shakspeare's self!
No head, save some world-genius, ought to rest
Above the treasures of that perfect breast,
Or nightly draw fresh light from those keen stars
Through which thy soul awes ours: yet thou art bound-
O waste of nature!-to a craven hound;
To shameless lust, and childish greed of pelf;
Athene to a Satyr: was that link
Forged by The Father's hand? Man's reason bars
The bans which God allowed.-Ay, so we think:
Forgetting, thou hadst weaker been, full blest,
Than thus made strong by suffering; and more great
In martyrdom, than throned as Caesar's mate.

The Bad Squire

The merry brown hares came leaping
Over the crest of the hill,
Where the clover and corn lay sleeping
Under the moonlight still.

Leaping late and early,
Till under their bite and their tread
The swedes and the wheat and the barley
Lay cankered and trampled and dead.

A poacher's widow sat sighing
On the side of the white chalk bank,
Where under the gloomy fir-woods
One spot in the ley throve rank.

She watched a long tuft of clover,
Where rabbit or hare never ran;
For its black sour haulm covered over
The blood of a murdered man.

She thought of the dark plantation,
And the hares, and her husband's blood,
And the voice of her indignation
Rose up to the throne of God.

'I am long past wailing and whining-
I have wept too much in my life:
I've had twenty years of pining
As an English labourer's wife.

'A labourer in Christian England,
Where they cant of a Saviour's name,
And yet waste men's lives like the vermin's
For a few more brace of game.

'There's blood on your new foreign shrubs, squire,
There's blood on your pointer's feet;
There's blood on the game you sell, squire,
And there's blood on the game you eat.

'You have sold the labouring-man, squire,
Body and soul to shame,
To pay for your seat in the House, squire,
And to pay for the feed of your game.

'You made him a poacher yourself, squire,
When you'd give neither work nor meat,
And your barley-fed hares robbed the garden
At our starving children's feet;

'When, packed in one reeking chamber,
Man, maid, mother, and little ones lay;
While the rain pattered in on the rotting bride-bed,
And the walls let in the day.

'When we lay in the burning fever
On the mud of the cold clay floor,
Till you parted us all for three months, squire,
At the dreary workhouse door.

'We quarrelled like brutes, and who wonders?
What self-respect could we keep,
Worse housed than your hacks and your pointers,
Worse fed than your hogs and your sheep?

'Our daughters with base-born babies
Have wandered away in their shame,
If your misses had slept, squire, where they did,
Your misses might do the same.

'Can your lady patch hearts that are breaking
With handfuls of coals and rice,

Or by dealing out flannel and sheeting
A little below cost price?

'You may tire of the jail and the workhouse,
And take to allotments and schools,
But you've run up a debt that will never
Be paid us by penny-club rules.

'In the season of shame and sadness,
In the dark and dreary day,
When scrofula, gout, and madness
Are eating your race away;

'When to kennels and liveried varlets
You have cast your daughter's bread,
And, worn out with liquor and harlots,
Your heir at your feet lies dead;

'When your youngest, the mealy-mouthed rector,
Lets your soul rot asleep to the grave,
You will find in your God the protector
Of the freeman you fancied your slave.'

She looked at the tuft of clover,
And wept till her heart grew light;
And at last, when her passion was over,
Went wandering into the night.

But the merry brown hares came leaping
Over the uplands still,
Where the clover and corn lay sleeping
On the side of the white chalk hill.

The Day of The Lord
The Day of the Lord is at hand, at hand:
Its storms roll up the sky:
The nations sleep starving on heaps of gold;
All dreamers toss and sigh;
The night is darkest before the morn;
When the pain is sorest the child is born,
And the Day of the Lord at hand.

Gather you, gather you, angels of God-
Freedom, and Mercy, and Truth;
Come! for the Earth is grown coward and old,
Come down, and renew us her youth.
Wisdom, Self-Sacrifice, Daring, and Love,
Haste to the battle-field, stoop from above,
To the Day of the Lord at hand.

Gather you, gather you, hounds of hell-

Famine, and Plague, and War;
Idleness, Bigotry, Cant, and Misrule,
Gather, and fall in the snare!
Hireling and Mammonite, Bigot and Knave,
Crawl to the battle-field, sneak to your grave,
In the Day of the Lord at hand.

Who would sit down and sigh for a lost age of gold,
While the Lord of all ages is here?
True hearts will leap up at the trumpet of God,
And those who can suffer, can dare.
Each old age of gold was an iron age too,
And the meekest of saints may find stern work to do,
In the Day of the Lord at hand.

The Dead Church

Wild wild wind, wilt thou never cease thy sighing?
Dark dark night, wilt thou never wear away?
Cold cold church, in thy death sleep lying,
The Lent is past, thy Passion here, but not thine Easter-day.

Peace, faint heart, though the night be dark and sighing;
Rest, fair corpse, where thy Lord himself hath lain.
Weep, dear Lord, above thy bride low lying;
Thy tears shall wake her frozen limbs to life and health again.

The Delectable Day

The boy on the famous gray pony,
Just bidding good-bye at the door,
Plucking up maiden heart for the fences
Where his brother won honour of yore.

The walk to 'the Meet' with fair children,
And women as gentle as gay,-
Ah! how do we male hogs in armour
Deserve such companions as they?

The afternoon's wander to windward,
To meet the dear boy coming back;
And to catch, down the turns of the valley,
The last weary chime of the pack.

The climb homeward by park and by moorland,
And through the fir forests again,
While the south-west wind roars in the gloaming,
Like an ocean of seething champagne.

And at night the septette of Beethoven,
And the grandmother by in her chair,
And the foot of all feet on the sofa

Beating delicate time to the air.

Ah, God! a poor soul can but thank Thee
For such a delectable day!
Though the fury, the fool, and the swindler,
To-morrow again have their way!

The Find

Yon sound's neither sheep-bell nor bark,
They're running-they're running, Go hark!
The sport may be lost by a moment's delay;
So whip up the puppies and scurry away.
Dash down through the cover by dingle and dell,
There's a gate at the bottom-I know it full well;
And they're running-they're running,
Go hark!

They're running-they're running, Go hark!
One fence and we're out of the park;
Sit down in your saddles and race at the brook,
Then smash at the bullfinch; no time for a look;
Leave cravens and skirters to dangle behind;
He's away for the moors in the teeth of the wind,
And they're running-they're running,
Go hark!

They're running-they're running, Go hark!
Let them run on and run till it's dark!
Well with them we are, and well with them we'll be,
While there's wind in our horses and daylight to see:
Then shog along homeward, chat over the fight,
And hear in our dreams the sweet music all night
Of-They're running-they're running,
Go hark!

The Invitation: To Tom Hughes

Come away with me, Tom,
Term and talk are done;
My poor lads are reaping,
Busy every one.
Curates mind the parish,
Sweepers mind the court;
We'll away to Snowdon
For our ten days' sport;
Fish the August evening
Till the eve is past,
Whoop like boys, at pounders
Fairly played and grassed.
When they cease to dimple,
Lunge, and swerve, and leap,

Then up over Siabod,
Choose our nest, and sleep.
Up a thousand feet, Tom,
Round the lion's head,
Find soft stones to leeward
And make up our bed.
Eat our bread and bacon,
Smoke the pipe of peace,
And, ere we be drowsy,
Give our boots a grease.
Homer's heroes did so,
Why not such as we?
What are sheets and servants?
Superfluity!
Pray for wives and children
Safe in slumber curled,
Then to chat till midnight
O'er this babbling world-
Of the workmen's college,
Of the price of grain,
Of the tree of knowledge,
Of the chance of rain;
If Sir A. goes Romeward,
If Miss B. sings true,
If the fleet comes homeward,
If the mare will do,-
Anything and everything-
Up there in the sky
Angels understand us,
And no 'saints' are by.
Down, and bathe at day-dawn,
Tramp from lake to lake,
Washing brain and heart clean
Every step we take.
Leave to Robert Browning
Beggars, fleas, and vines;
Leave to mournful Ruskin
Popish Apennines,
Dirty Stones of Venice
And his Gas-lamps Seven-
We've the stones of Snowdon
And the lamps of heaven.
Where's the mighty credit
In admiring Alps?
Any goose sees 'glory'
In their 'snowy scalps.'
Leave such signs and wonders
For the dullard brain,
As aesthetic brandy,
Opium and cayenne.
Give me Bramshill common
(St. John's harriers by),

Or the vale of Windsor,
England's golden eye.
Show me life and progress,
Beauty, health, and man;
Houses fair, trim gardens,
Turn where'er I can.
Or, if bored with 'High Art,'
And such popish stuff,
One's poor ear need airing,
Snowdon's high enough.
While we find God's signet
Fresh on English ground,
Why go gallivanting
With the nations round?
Though we try no ventures
Desperate or strange;
Feed on commonplaces
In a narrow range;
Never sought for Franklin
Round the frozen Capes;
Even, with Macdougall,
Bagged our brace of apes;
Never had our chance, Tom,
In that black Redan;
Can't avenge poor Brereton
Out in Sakarran;
Tho' we earn our bread, Tom,
By the dirty pen,
What we can we will be,
Honest Englishmen.
Do the work that's nearest,
Though it's dull at whiles,
Helping, when we meet them,
Lame dogs over stiles;
See in every hedgerow
Marks of angels' feet,
Epics in each pebble
Underneath our feet;
Once a year, like schoolboys,
Robin-Hooding go,
Leaving fops and fogies
A thousand feet below.

The Knight's Leap: A Legend of Altenar
'So the foemen have fired the gate, men of mine;
And the water is spent and gone?
Then bring me a cup of the red Ahr-wine:
I never shall drink but this one.

'And reach me my harness, and saddle my horse,
And lead him me round to the door:

He must take such a leap to-night perforce,
As horse never took before.

'I have fought my fight, I have lived my life,
I have drunk my share of wine;
From Trier to Coln there was never a knight
Led a merrier life than mine.

'I have lived by the saddle for years two score;
And if I must die on tree,
Then the old saddle tree, which has borne me of yore,
Is the properest timber for me.

'So now to show bishop, and burgher, and priest,
How the Altenahr hawk can die:
If they smoke the old falcon out of his nest,
He must take to his wings and fly.'

He harnessed himself by the clear moonshine,
And he mounted his horse at the door;
And he drained such a cup of the red Ahr-wine,
As man never drained before.

He spurred the old horse, and he held him tight,
And he leapt him out over the wall;
Out over the cliff, out into the night,
Three hundred feet of fall.

They found him next morning below in the glen,
With never a bone in him whole-
A mass or a prayer, now, good gentlemen,
For such a bold rider's soul.

The Knight's Return
Hark! hark! hark!
The lark sings high in the dark.
The were wolves mutter, the night hawks moan,
The raven croaks from the Raven-stone;
What care I for his boding groan,
Riding the moorland to come to mine own?
Hark! hark! hark!
The lark sings high in the dark.

Hark! hark! hark!
The lark sings high in the dark.
Long have I wander'd by land and by sea,
Long have I ridden by moorland and lea;
Yonder she sits with my babe on her knee,
Sits at the window and watches for me!
Hark! hark! hark!
The lark sings high in the dark.

The Last Buccaneer

OH, England is a pleasant place for them that 's rich and high;
But England is a cruel place for such poor folks as I;
And such a port for mariners I ne'er shall see again,
As the pleasant Isle of Avès, beside the Spanish main.

There were forty craft in Avès that were both swift and stout,
All furnish'd well with small arms and cannons round about;
And a thousand men in Avès made laws so fair and free
To choose their valiant captains and obey them loyally.

Thence we sail'd against the Spaniard with his hoards of plate and gold,
Which he wrung by cruel tortures from the Indian folk of old;
Likewise the merchant captains, with hearts as hard as stone,
Which flog men and keelhaul them and starve them to the bone.

Oh, the palms grew high in Avès and fruits that shone like gold,
And the colibris and parrots they were gorgeous to behold;
And the negro maids to Avès from bondage fast did flee,
To welcome gallant sailors a sweeping in from sea.

Oh, sweet it was in Avès to hear the landward breeze
A-swing with good tobacco in a net between the trees,
With a negro lass to fan you while you listen'd to the roar
Of the breakers on the reef outside that never touched the shore.

But Scripture saith, an ending to all fine things must be,
So the King's ships sail'd on Avès and quite put down were we.
All day we fought like bulldogs, but they burst the booms at night;
And I fled in a piragua sore wounded from the fight.

Nine days I floated starving, and a negro lass beside,
Till for all I tried to cheer her, the poor young thing she died;
But as I lay a gasping a Bristol sail came by,
And brought me home to England here to beg until I die.
And now I 'm old and going I 'm sure I can't tell where;
One comfort is, this world's so hard I can't be worse off there:
If I might but be a sea-dove I 'd fly across the main,
To the pleasant Isle of Avès, to look at it once again.

The Legend of La Brea

Down beside the loathly Pitch Lake,
In the stately Morichal,
Sat an ancient Spanish Indian,
Peering through the columns tall.

Watching vainly for the flashing
Of the jewelled colibris;

Listening vainly for their humming
Round the honey-blossomed trees.

'Few,' he sighed, 'they come, and fewer,
To the cocorite bowers;
Murdered, madly, through the forests
Which of yore were theirs-and ours

By there came a negro hunter,
Lithe and lusty, sleek and strong,
Rolling round his sparkling eyeballs,
As he loped and lounged along.

Rusty firelock on his shoulder;
Rusty cutlass on his thigh;
Never jollier British subject
Rollicked underneath the sky.

British law to give him safety,
British fleets to guard his shore,
And a square of British freehold-
He had all we have, and more.

Fattening through the endless summer,
Like his own provision ground,
He had reached the summum bonum
Which our latest wits have found.

So he thought; and in his hammock
Gnawed his junk of sugar-cane,
Toasted plantains at the fire-stick,
Gnawed, and dozed, and gnawed again.

Had a wife in his ajoupa -
Or, at least, what did instead;
Children, too, who died so early,
He'd no need to earn their bread.

Never stole, save what he needed,
From the Crown woods round about;
Never lied, except when summoned-
Let the warden find him out.

Never drank, except at market;
Never beat his sturdy mate;
She could hit as hard as he could,
And had just as hard a pate.

Had no care for priest nor parson,
Hope of heaven nor fear of hell;
And in all his views of nature
Held with Comte and Peter Bell.

Healthy, happy, silly, kindly,
Neither care nor toil had he,
Save to work an hour at sunrise,
And then hunt the colibri.

Not a bad man; not a good man:
Scarce a man at all, one fears,
If the Man be that within us
Which is born of fire and tears.

Round the palm-stems, round the creepers,
Flashed a feathered jewel past,
Ruby-crested, topaz-throated,
Plucked the cocorite bast,

Plucked the fallen ceiba-cotton,
Whirred away to build his nest,
Hung at last, with happy humming,
Round some flower he fancied best.

Up then went the rusty muzzle,
'Dat de tenth I shot to-day:'
But out sprang the Indian shouting,
Balked the negro of his prey.

'Eh, you Senor Trinidada!
What dis new ondacent plan?
Spoil a genl'man's chance ob shooting?
I as good as any man.

'Dese not your woods; dese de Queen's woods:
You seem not know whar you ar,
Gibbin' yuself dese buckra airs here,
You black Indian Papist! Dar!'

Stately, courteous, stood the Indian;
Pointed through the palm-tree shade:
'Does the gentleman of colour
Know how yon Pitch Lake was made?'

Grinned the negro, grinned and trembled-
Through his nerves a shudder ran-
Saw a snake-like eye that held him;
Saw-he'd met an Obeah man.

Saw a fetish-such a bottle-
Buried at his cottage door;
Toad and spider, dirty water,
Rusty nails, and nine charms more.

Saw in vision such a cock's head

In the path-and it was white!
Saw Brinvilliers in his pottage:
Faltered, cold and damp with fright.

Fearful is the chance of poison:
Fearful, too, the great unknown:
Magic brings some positivists
Humbly on their marrow-bone.

Like the wedding-guest enchanted,
There he stood, a trembling cur;
While the Indian told his story,
Like the Ancient Mariner.

Told how-'Once that loathly Pitch Lake
Was a garden bright and fair;
How the Chaymas off the mainland
Built their palm ajoupas there.

'How they throve, and how they fattened,
Hale and happy, safe and strong;
Passed the livelong days in feasting;
Passed the nights in dance and song.

'Till they cruel grew, and wanton:
Till they killed the colibris.
Then outspake the great Good Spirit,
Who can see through all the trees,

'Said-'And what have I not sent you,
Wanton Chaymas, many a year?
Lapp, agouti, cachicame,
Quenc and guazu-pita deer.

"Fish I sent you, sent you turtle,
Chip-chip, conch, flamingo red,
Woodland paui, horned screamer,
And blue ramier overhead.

"Plums from balata and mombin,
Tania, manioc, water-vine;
Let you fell my slim manacques,
Tap my sweet moriche wine.

"Sent rich plantains, food of angels;
Rich ananas, food of kings;
Grudged you none of all my treasures:
Save these lovely useless things.'

'But the Chaymas' ears were deafened;
Blind their eyes, and could not see
How a blissful Indian's spirit

Lived in every colibri.

'Lived, forgetting toil and sorrow,
Ever fair and ever new;
Whirring round the dear old woodland,
Feeding on the honey-dew.

'Till one evening roared the earthquake:
Monkeys howled, and parrots screamed:
And the Guaraons at morning
Gathered here, as men who dreamed.

'Sunk were gardens, sunk ajoupas;
Hut and hammock, man and hound:
And above the Chayma village
Boiled with pitch the cursed ground.

'Full, and too full; safe, and too safe;
Negro man, take care, take care.
He that wantons with God's bounties
Of God's wrath had best beware.

'For the saucy, reckless, heartless,
Evil days are sure in store.
You may see the Negro sinking
As the Chayma sank of yore.'

Loudly laughed that stalwart hunter-
'Eh, what superstitious talk!
Nyam am nyam, an' maney maney;
Birds am birds, like park am park;
An' dere's twenty thousand birdskins
Ardered jes' now fram New Yark.'

The Song of The Little Baltung: A.D. 395

A harper came over the Danube so wide,
And he came into Alaric's hall,
And he sang the song of the little Baltung
To him and his heroes all.

How the old old Balt and the young young Balt
Rode out of Caucaland,
With the royal elephant's trunk on helm
And the royal lance in hand.

Thuringer heroes, counts and knights,
Pricked proud in their meinie;
For they were away to the great Kaiser,
In Byzant beside the sea.

And when they came to the Danube so wide

They shouted from off the shore,
'Come over, come over, ye Roman slaves,
And ferry your masters o'er.'

And when they came to Adrian's burgh,
With its towers so smooth and high,
'Come out, come out, ye Roman knaves,
And see your lords ride by.'

But when they came lo the long long walls
That stretch from sea to sea,
That old old Balt let down his chin,
And a thoughtful man grew he.

'Oh oft have I scoffed at brave Fridigern,
But never will I scoff more,
If these be the walls which kept him out
From the Micklegard there on the shore.'

Then out there came the great Kaiser,
With twice ten thousand men;
But never a Thuring was coward enough
To wish himself home again.

'Bow down, thou rebel, old Athanarich,
And beg thy life this day;
The Kaiser is lord of all the world,
And who dare say him nay?'

'I never came out of Caucaland
To beg for less nor more;
But to see the pride of the great Kaiser,
In his Micklegard here by the shore.

'I never came out of Caucaland
To bow to mortal wight,
But to shake the hand of the great Kaiser,
And God defend my right.'

He shook his hand, that cunning Kaiser,
And he kissed him courteouslie,
And he has ridden with Athanarich
That wonder-town to see.

He showed him his walls of marble white-
A mile o'erhead they shone;
Quoth the Balt, 'Who would leap into that garden,
King Siegfried's boots must own.'

He showed him his engines of arsmetrick
And his wells of quenchless flame,
And his flying rocks, that guarded his walls

From all that against him came.

He showed him his temples and pillared halls,
And his streets of houses high;
And his watch-towers tall, where his star-gazers
Sit reading the signs of the sky.

He showed him his ships with their hundred oars,
And their sides like a castle wall,
That fetch home the plunder of all the world,
At the Kaiser's beck and call.

He showed him all nations of every tongue
That are bred beneath the sun,
How they flowed together in Micklegard street
As the brooks flow all into one.

He showed him the shops of the china ware,
And of silk and sendal also,
And he showed him the baths and the waterpipes
On arches aloft that go.

He showed him ostrich and unicorn,
Ape, lion, and tiger keen;
And elephants wise roared 'Hail Kaiser!'
As though they had Christians been.

He showed him the hoards of the dragons and trolls,
Rare jewels and heaps of gold-
'Hast thou seen, in all thy hundred years,
Such as these, thou king so old?'

Now that cunning Kaiser was a scholar wise,
And could of gramarye,
And he cast a spell on that old old Balt,
Till lowly and meek spake he.

'Oh oft have I heard of the Micklegard,
What I held for chapmen's lies;
But now do I know of the Micklegard,
By the sight of mine own eyes.

'Woden in Valhalla,
But thou on earth art God;
And he that dare withstand thee, Kaiser,
On his own head lies his blood.'

Then out and spake that little Baltung,
Rode at the king's right knee,
Quoth 'Fridigern slew false Kaiser Valens,
And he died like you or me.'

'And who art thou, thou pretty bold boy,
Rides at the king's right knee?'
'Oh I am the Baltung, boy Alaric,
And as good a man as thee.'

'As good as me, thou pretty bold boy,
With down upon thy chin?'
'Oh a spae-wife laid a doom on me,
The best of thy realm to win.'

'If thou be so fierce, thou little wolf cub
Or ever thy teeth be grown;
Then I must guard my two young sons
Lest they should lose their own.'

'Oh, it's I will guard your two lither lads,
In their burgh beside the sea,
And it's I will prove true man to them
If they will prove true to me.

'But it's you must warn your two lither lads,
And warn them bitterly,
That if I shall find them two false Kaisers,
High hanged they both shall be.'

Now they are gone into the Kaiser's palace
To eat the peacock fine,
And they are gone into the Kaiser's palace
To drink the good Greek wine.

The Kaiser alone, and the old old Balt,
They sat at the cedar board;
And round them served on the bended knee
Full many a Roman lord.

'What ails thee, what ails thee, friend Athanarich?
What makes thee look so pale?'
'I fear I am poisoned, thou cunning Kaiser,
For I feel my heart-strings fail.

'Oh would I had kept that great great oath
I swore by the horse's head,
I would never set foot on Roman ground
Till the day that I lay dead.

'Oh would I were home in Caucaland,
To hear my harpers play,
And to drink my last of the nut-brown ale,
While I gave the gold rings away.

'Oh would I were home in Caucaland,
To hear the Gothmen's horn,

And watch the waggons, and brown brood mares
And the tents where I was born.

'But now I must die between four stone walls
In Byzant beside the sea:
And as thou shalt deal with my little Baltung,
So God shall deal with thee.'

The Kaiser he purged himself with oaths,
And he buried him royally,
And he set on his barrow an idol of gold,
Where all Romans must bow the knee.

And now the Goths are the Kaiser's men,
And guard him with lance and sword,
And the little Baltung is his sworn son-at-arms,
And eats at the Kaiser's board,

And the Kaiser's two sons are two false white lads
That a clerk may beat with cane.
The clerk that should beat that little Baltung
Would never sing mass again.

Oh the gates of Rome they are steel without,
And beaten gold within:
But they shall fly wide to the little Baltung
With the down upon his chin.

Oh the fairest flower in the Kaiser's garden
Is Rome and Italian land:
But it all shall fall to the little Baltung
When he shall take lance in hand.

And when he is parting the plunder of Rome,
He shall pay for this song of mine,
Neither maiden nor land, neither jewel nor gold,
But one cup of Italian wine.

The Longbeard's Saga: A.D. 400
Over the camp-fires
Drank I with heroes,
Under the Donau bank,
Warm in the snow trench:
Sagamen heard I there,
Men of the Longbeards,
Cunning and ancient,
Honey-sweet-voiced.
Scaring the wolf cub,
Scaring the horn-owl,
Shaking the snow-wreaths
Down from the pine-boughs,

Up to the star roof
Rang out their song.
Singing how Winil men,
Over the ice-floes
Sledging from Scanland
Came unto Scoring;
Singing of Gambara,
Freya's beloved,
Mother of Ayo,
Mother of Ibor.
Singing of Wendel men,
Ambri and Assi;
How to the Winilfolk
Went they with war-words,
'Few are ye, strangers,
And many are we:
Pay us now toll and fee,
Cloth-yarn, and rings, and beeves:
Else at the raven's meal
Bide the sharp bill's doom.'
Clutching the dwarfs work then,
Clutching the bullock's shell,
Girding gray iron on,
Forth fared the Winils all,
Fared the Alruna's sons,
Ayo and Ibor.
Mad at heart stalked they:
Loud wept the women all,
Loud the Alruna wife;
Sore was their need.
Out of the morning land,
Over the snow-drifts,
Beautiful Freya came,
Tripping to Scoring.
White were the moorlands,
And frozen before her:
Green were the moorlands,
And blooming behind her.
Out of her gold locks
Shaking the spring flowers,
Out of her garments
Shaking the south wind,
Around in the birches
Awaking the throstles,
And making chaste housewives all
Long for their heroes home,
Loving and love-giving,
Came she to Scoring.
Came unto Gambara,
Wisest of Valas,
'Vala, why weepest thou?
Far in the wide-blue,

High up in the Elfin-home,
Heard I thy weeping.'
'Stop not my weeping,
Till one can fight seven.
Sons have I, heroes tall,
First in the sword-play;
This day at the Wendels' hands
Eagles must tear them.
Their mothers, thrall-weary,
Must grind for the Wendels.'
Wept the Alruna wife;
Kissed her fair Freya:-
'Far off in the morning land,
High in Valhalla,
A window stands open;
Its sill is the snow-peaks,
Its posts are the waterspouts,
Storm-rack its lintel;
Gold cloud-flakes above
Are piled for the roofing,
Far up to the Elfin-home,
High in the wide-blue.
Smiles out each morning thence
Odin Allfather;
From under the cloud-eaves
Smiles out on the heroes,
Smiles on chaste housewives all,
Smiles on the brood-mares,
Smiles on the smiths' work:
And theirs is the sword-luck,
With them is the glory,
So Odin hath sworn it,
Who first in the morning
Shall meet him and greet him.'
Still the Alruna wept:-
'Who then shall greet him?
Women alone are here:
Far on the moorlands
Behind the war-lindens,
In vain for the bill's doom
Watch Winil heroes all,
One against seven.'
Sweetly the Queen laughed:-
'Hear thou my counsel now;
Take to thee cunning,
Beloved of Freya.
Take thou thy women-folk,
Maidens and wives:
Over your ankles
Lace on the white war-hose;
Over your bosoms
Link up the hard mail-nets;

Over your lips
Plait long tresses with cunning;-
So war-beasts full-bearded
King Odin shall deem you,
When off the gray sea-beach
At sunrise ye greet him.'

Night's son was driving
His golden-haired horses up;
Over the eastern firths
High flashed their manes.
Smiled from the cloud-eaves out
Allfather Odin,
Waiting the battle-sport:
Freya stood by him.
'Who are these heroes tall,
Lusty-limbed Longbeards?
Over the swans' bath
Why cry they to me?
Bones should be crashing fast,
Wolves should be full-fed,
Where such, mad-hearted,
Swing hands in the sword-play.'

Sweetly laughed Freya:-
'A name thou hast given them,
Shames neither thee nor them,
Well can they wear it.
Give them the victory,
First have they greeted thee;
Give them the victory,
Yokefellow mine!
Maidens and wives are these,
Wives of the Winils;
Few are their heroes
And far on the war-road,
So over the swans' bath
They cry unto thee.'

Royally laughed he then;
Dear was that craft to him,
Odin Allfather,
Shaking the clouds.
'Cunning are women all,
Bold and importunate!
Longbeards their name shall be,
Ravens shall thank them:
Where women are heroes,
What must the men be?
Theirs is the victory;
No need of me!'

The Mango-Tree

He wiled me through the furzy croft;
He wiled me down the sandy lane.
He told his boy's love, soft and oft,
Until I told him mine again.

We married, and we sailed the main;
A soldier, and a soldier's wife.
We marched through many a burning plain;
We sighed for many a gallant life.

But his-God kept it safe from harm.
He toiled, and dared, and earned command;
And those three stripes upon his arm
Were more to me than gold or land.

Sure he would win some great renown:
Our lives were strong, our hearts were high.
One night the fever struck him down.
I sat, and stared, and saw him die.

I had his children-one, two, three.
One week I had them, blithe and sound.
The next-beneath this mango-tree,
By him in barrack burying-ground.

I sit beneath the mango-shade;
I live my five years' life all o'er-
Round yonder stems his children played;
He mounted guard at yonder door.

'Tis I, not they, am gone and dead.
They live; they know; they feel; they see.
Their spirits light the golden shade
Beneath the giant mango-tree.

All things, save I, are full of life:
The minas, pluming velvet breasts;
The monkeys, in their foolish strife;
The swooping hawks, the swinging nests;

The lizards basking on the soil,
The butterflies who sun their wings;
The bees about their household toil,
They live, they love, the blissful things.

Each tender purple mango-shoot,
That folds and droops so bashful down;
It lives; it sucks some hidden root;
It rears at last a broad green crown.

It blossoms; and the children cry-
'Watch when the mango-apples fall.'
It lives: but rootless, fruitless, I-
I breathe and dream;-and that is all.

Thus am I dead: yet cannot die:
But still within my foolish brain
There hangs a pale blue evening sky;
A furzy croft; a sandy lane.

The Night Bird: A Myth
A floating, a floating
Across the sleeping sea,
All night I heard a singing bird
Upon the topmost tree.

'Oh came you off the isles of Greece,
Or off the banks of Seine;
Or off some tree in forests free,
Which fringe the western main?'

'I came not off the old world
Nor yet from off the new-
But I am one of the birds of God
Which sing the whole night through.'

'Oh sing, and wake the dawning-
Oh whistle for the wind;
The night is long, the current strong,
My boat it lags behind.'

'The current sweeps the old world,
The current sweeps the new;
The wind will blow, the dawn will glow
Ere thou hast sailed them through.'

The Old, Old Song
When all the world is young, lad,
And all the trees are green;
And every goose a swan, lad,
And every lass a queen—
Then hey for boot and horse lad,
And round the world away;
Young blood must have its course, lad,
And every dog his day.

When all the world is old, lad,
And all the trees are brown;
And all the sport is stale, lad,
And all the wheels run down—

Creep home, and take your place there,
The spent and manned among;
God grant you find one face there
You loved when all was young.

The Oubit

It was an hairy oubit, sae proud he crept alang,
A feckless hairy oubit, and merrily he sang-
'My Minnie bad me bide at hame until I won my wings;
I show her soon my soul's aboon the warks o' creeping things.'

This feckless hairy oubit cam' hirpling by the linn,
A swirl o' wind cam' doun the glen, and blew that oubit in:
Oh when he took the water, the saumon fry they rose,
And tigg'd him a' to pieces sma', by head and tail and toes.

Tak' warning then, young poets a', by this poor oubit's shame;
Though Pegasus may nicher loud, keep Pegasus at hame.
Oh haud your hands frae inkhorns, though a' the Muses woo;
For critics lie, like saumon fry, to mak' their meals o' you.

The Outlaw

Oh, I wadna be a yeoman, mither, to follow my father's trade,
To bow my back in miry banks, at pleugh and hoe and spade.
Stinting wife, and bairns, and kye, to fat some courtier lord,-
Let them die o' rent wha like, mither, and I'll die by sword.

Nor I wadna be a clerk, mither, to bide aye ben,
Scrabbling ower the sheets o' parchment with a weary weary pen;
Looking through the lang stane windows at a narrow strip o' sky,
Like a laverock in a withy cage, until I pine away and die.

Nor I wadna be a merchant, mither, in his lang furred gown,
Trailing strings o' footsore horses through the noisy dusty town;
Louting low to knights and ladies, fumbling o'er his wares,
Telling lies, and scraping siller, heaping cares on cares.

Nor I wadna be a soldier, mither, to dice wi' ruffian bands,
Pining weary months in castles, looking over wasted lands.
Smoking byres, and shrieking women, and the grewsome sights o' war-
There's blood on my hand eneugh, mither; it's ill to make it mair.

If I had married a wife, mither, I might ha' been douce and still,
And sat at hame by the ingle side to crack and laugh my fill;
Sat at hame wi' the woman I looed, and wi' bairnies at my knee:
But death is bauld, and age is cauld, and luve's no for me.

For when first I stirred in your side, mither, ye ken full well
How you lay all night up among the deer out on the open fell;
And so it was that I won the heart to wander far and near,

Caring neither for land nor lassie, but the bonnie dun deer.

Yet I am not a losel and idle, mither, nor a thief that steals;
I do but hunt God's cattle, upon God's ain hills;
For no man buys and sells the deer, and the bonnie fells are free
To a belted knight with hawk on hand, and a gangrel loon like me.

So I'm aff and away to the muirs, mither, to hunt the deer,
Ranging far frae frowning faces, and the douce folk here;
Crawling up through burn and bracken, louping down the screes,
Looking out frae craig and headland, drinking up the simmer breeze.

Oh, the wafts o' heather honey, and the music o' the brae,
As I watch the great harts feeding, nearer, nearer a' the day.
Oh, to hark the eagle screaming, sweeping, ringing round the sky-
That's a bonnier life than stumbling ower the muck to colt and kye.

And when I'm taen and hangit, mither, a brittling o' my deer,
Ye'll no leave your bairn to the corbie craws, to dangle in the air;
But ye'll send up my twa douce brethren, and ye'll steal me frae the tree,
And bury me up on the brown brown muirs, where I aye looed to be.

Ye'll bury me 'twixt the brae and the burn, in a glen far away,
Where I may hear the heathcock craw, and the great harts bray;
And gin my ghaist can walk, mither, I'll go glowering at the sky,
The livelong night on the black hill sides where the dun deer lie.

The Poetry of A Root Crop
Underneath their eider-robe
Russet swede and golden globe,
Feathered carrot, burrowing deep,
Steadfast wait in charmed sleep;
Treasure-houses wherein lie,
Locked by angels' alchemy,
Milk and hair, and blood, and bone,
Children of the barren stone;
Children of the flaming Air,
With his blue eye keen and bare,
Spirit-peopled smiling down
On frozen field and toiling town-
Toiling town that will not heed
God His voice for rage and greed;
Frozen fields that surpliced lie,
Gazing patient at the sky;
Like some marble carven nun,
With folded hands when work is done,
Who mute upon her tomb doth pray,
Till the resurrection day.

The Priest's Heart

It was Sir John, the fair young Priest,
He strode up off the strand;
But seven fisher maidens he left behind
All dancing hand in hand.

He came unto the wise wife's house:
'Now, Mother, to prove your art;
To charm May Carleton's merry blue eyes
Out of a young man's heart.'

'My son, you went for a holy man,
Whose heart was set on high;
Go sing in your psalter, and read in your books;
Man's love fleets lightly by.'

'I had liever to talk with May Carleton,
Than with all the saints in Heaven;
I had liever to sit by May Carleton
Than climb the spheres seven.

'I have watched and fasted, early and late,
I have prayed to all above;
But I find no cure save churchyard mould
For the pain which men call love.'

'Now Heaven forefend that ill grow worse:
Enough that ill be ill.
I know of a spell to draw May Carleton,
And bend her to your will.'

'If thou didst that which thou canst not do,
Wise woman though thou be,
I would run and run till I buried myself
In the surge of yonder sea.

'Scathless for me are maid and wife,
And scathless shall they bide.
Yet charm me May Carleton's eyes from the heart
That aches in my left side.'

She charmed him with the white witchcraft,
She charmed him with the black,
But he turned his fair young face to the wall,
Till she heard his heart-strings crack.

The Red King

The King was drinking in Malwood Hall,
There came in a monk before them all:
He thrust by squire, he thrust by knight,
Stood over against the dais aright;

And, 'The word of the Lord, thou cruel Red King,
The word of the Lord to thee I bring.
A grimly sweven I dreamt yestreen;
I saw thee lie under the hollins green,
And through thine heart an arrow keen;
And out of thy body a smoke did rise,
Which smirched the sunshine out of the skies:
So if thou God's anointed be
I rede thee unto thy soul thou see.
For mitre and pall thou hast y-sold,
False knight to Christ, for gain and gold;
And for this thy forest were digged down all,
Steading and hamlet and churches tall;
And Christes poor were ousten forth,
To beg their bread from south to north.
So tarry at home, and fast and pray,
Lest fiends hunt thee in the judgment-day.'

The monk he vanished where he stood;
King William sterte up wroth and wood;
Quod he, 'Fools' wits will jump together;
The Hampshire ale and the thunder weather
Have turned the brains for us both, I think;
And monks are curst when they fall to drink.
A lothly sweven I dreamt last night,
How there hoved anigh me a griesly knight,
Did smite me down to the pit of hell;
I shrieked and woke, so fast I fell.
There's Tyrrel as sour as I, perdie,
So he of you all shall hunt with me;
A grimly brace for a hart to see.'

The Red King down from Malwood came;
His heart with wine was all aflame,
His eyne were shotten, red as blood,
He rated and swore, wherever he rode.
They roused a hart, that grimly brace,
A hart of ten, a hart of grease,
Fled over against the kinges place.
The sun it blinded the kinges ee,
A fathom behind his hocks shot he:
'Shoot thou,' quod he, 'in the fiendes name,
To lose such a quarry were seven years' shame.'
And he hove up his hand to mark the game.
Tyrrel he shot full light, God wot;
For whether the saints they swerved the shot,
'Or whether by treason, men knowen not,
But under the arm, in a secret part,
The iron fled through the kinges heart.
The turf it squelched where the Red King fell;
And the fiends they carried his soul to hell,
Quod 'His master's name it hath sped him well.'

Tyrrel he smiled full grim that day,
Quod 'Shooting of kings is no bairns' play;'
And he smote in the spurs, and fled fast away.
As he pricked along by Fritham plain,
The green tufts flew behind like rain;
The waters were out, and over the sward:
He swam his horse like a stalwart lord:
Men clepen that water Tyrrel's ford.
By Rhinefield and by Osmondsleigh,
Through glade and furze brake fast drove he,
Until he heard the roaring sea;
Quod he, 'Those gay waves they call me.'
By Mary's grace a seely boat
On Christchurch bar did lie afloat;
He gave the shipmen mark and groat,
To ferry him over to Normandie,
And there he fell to sanctuarie;
God send his soul all bliss to see.

And fend our princes every one,
From foul mishap and trahison;
But kings that harrow Christian men
Shall England never bide again.

The Sands of Dee
"O Mary, go and call the cattle home,
And call the cattle home,
And call the cattle home
Across the sands of Dee";
The western wind was wild and dank with foam,
And all alone went she.

The western tide crept up along the sand,
And o'er and o'er the sand,
And round and round the sand,
As far as eye could see.
The rolling mist came down and hid the land:
And never home came she.

"Oh! is it weed, or fish, or floating hair
A tress of golden hair,
A drownèd maiden's hair
Above the nets at sea?
Was never salmon yet that shone so fair
Among the stakes on Dee."

They rowed her in across the rolling foam,
The cruel crawling foam,
The cruel hungry foam,
To her grave beside the sea:

But still the boatmen hear her call the cattle home
Across the sands of Dee.

The South Wind: A Fisherman's Blessing
O blessed drums of Aldershot!
O blessed South-west train!
O blessed, blessed Speaker's clock,
All prophesying rain!

O blessed yaffil, laughing loud!
O blessed falling glass!
O blessed fan of cold gray cloud!
O blessed smelling grass!

O bless'd South wind that toots his horn
Through every hole and crack!
I'm off at eight to-morrow morn,
To bring
such
fishes back!

The Starlings
Early in spring time, on raw and windy mornings,
Beneath the freezing house-eaves I heard the starlings sing-
'Ah dreary March month, is this then a time for building wearily?
Sad, sad, to think that the year is but begun.'

Late in the autumn, on still and cloudless evenings,
Among the golden reed-beds I heard the starlings sing-
'Ah that sweet March month, when we and our mates were courting merrily;
Sad, sad, to think that the year is all but done.'

The Summer Sea
Soft soft wind, from out the sweet south sliding,
Waft thy silver cloud webs athwart the summer sea;
Thin thin threads of mist on dewy fingers twining
Weave a veil of dappled gauze to shade my babe and me.

Deep deep Love, within thine own abyss abiding,
Pour Thyself abroad, O Lord, on earth and air and sea;
Worn weary hearts within Thy holy temple hiding,
Shield from sorrow, sin, and shame my helpless babe and me.

The Swan-Neck
Evil sped the battle play
On the Pope Calixtus' day;
Mighty war-smiths, thanes and lords,
In Senlac slept the sleep of swords.

Harold Earl, shot over shield,
Lay along the autumn weald;
Slaughter such was never none
Since the Ethelings England won.
Thither Lady Githa came,
Weeping sore for grief and shame;
How may she her first-born tell?
Frenchmen stript him where he fell,
Gashed and marred his comely face;
Who can know him in his place?
Up and spake two brethren wise,
'Youngest hearts have keenest eyes;
Bird which leaves its mother's nest,
Moults its pinions, moults its crest.
Let us call the Swan-neck here,
She that was his leman dear;
She shall know him in this stound;
Foot of wolf, and scent of hound,
Eye of hawk, and wing of dove,
Carry woman to her love.'
Up and spake the Swan-neck high,
'Go! to all your thanes let cry
How I loved him best of all,
I whom men his leman call;
Better knew his body fair
Than the mother which him bare.
When ye lived in wealth and glee
Then ye scorned to look on me;
God hath brought the proud ones low
After me afoot to go.'
Rousing erne and sallow glede,
Rousing gray wolf off his feed,
Over franklin, earl, and thane,
Heaps of mother-naked slain,
Round the red field tracing slow,
Stooped that Swan-neck white as snow;
Never blushed nor turned away,
Till she found him where he lay;
Clipt him in her armes fair,
Wrapt him in her yellow hair,
Bore him from the battle-stead,
Saw him laid in pall of lead,
Took her to a minster high,
For Earl Harold's soul to cry.

Thus fell Harold, bracelet-giver;
Jesu rest his soul for ever;
Angles all from thrall deliver;
Miserere Domine.

The Three Fishers

Three fishers went sailing away to the west,
Away to the west as the sun went down;
Each thought on the woman who loved him the best,
And the children stood watching them out of the town;
For men must work, and women must weep,
And there's little to earn, and many to keep,
Though the harbour bar be moaning.

Three wives sat up in the lighthouse tower,
And they trimmed the lamps as the sun went down;
They looked at the squall, and they looked at the shower,
And the night-rack came rolling up ragged and brown.
But men must work, and women must weep,
Though storms be sudden, and waters deep,
And the harbour bar be moaning.

Three corpses lay out on the shining sands
In the morning gleam as the tide went down,
And the women are weeping and wringing their hands
For those who will never come home to the town;
For men must work, and women must weep,
And the sooner it's over, the sooner to sleep;
And good-bye to the bar and its moaning.

The Tide River
Clear and cool, clear and cool,
By laughing shallow and dreaming pool;
Cool and clear, cool and clear,
By shining shingle and foaming weir;
Under the crag where the ouzel sings,
And the ivied wall where the church-bell rings,
Undefiled, for the undefiled;
Play by me, bathe in me, mother and child.

Dank and foul, dank and foul,
By the smoky town in its murky cowl;
Foul and dank, foul and dank,
By wharf and sewer and slimy bank;
Darker and darker the farther I go,
Baser and baser the richer I grow;
Who dare sport with the sin-defiled?
Shrink from me, turn from me, mother and child.

Strong and free, strong and free,
The flood-gates are open, away to the sea.
Free and strong, free and strong,
Cleansing my streams as I hurry along,
To the golden sands, and the leaping bar,
And the taintless tide that awaits me afar.
As I lose myself in the infinite main,
Like a soul that has sinned and is pardoned again,

Undefiled, for the undefiled;
Play by me, bathe in me, mother and child.

The Tide Rock

How sleeps yon rock, whose half-day's bath is done.
With broad blight side beneath the broad bright sun,
Like sea-nymph tired, on cushioned mosses sleeping.
Yet, nearer drawn, beneath her purple tresses
From drooping brows we find her slowly weeping.
So many a wife for cruel man's caresses
Must inly pine and pine, yet outward bear
A gallant front to this world's gaudy glare.

The Ugly Princess

My parents bow, and lead them forth,
For all the crowd to see-
Ah well! the people might not care
To cheer a dwarf like me.

They little know how I could love,
How I could plan and toil,
To swell those drudges' scanty gains,
Their mites of rye and oil.

They little know what dreams have been
My playmates, night and day;
Of equal kindness, helpful care,
A mother's perfect sway.

Now earth to earth in convent walls,
To earth in churchyard sod:
I was not good enough for man,
And so am given to God.

The Watchman

'Watchman, what of the night?'
'The stars are out in the sky;
And the merry round moon will be rising soon,
For us to go sailing by.'

'Watchman, what of the night?'
'The tide flows in from the sea;
There's water to float a little cockboat
Will carry such fishers as we.'

'Watchman, what of the night?'
'The night is a fruitful time;
When to many a pair are born children fair,
To be christened at morning chime.'

The Weird Lady

The swevens came up round Harold the Earl,
Like motes in the sunnes beam;
And over him stood the Weird Lady,
In her charmed castle over the sea,
Sang 'Lie thou still and dream.'

'Thy steed is dead in his stall, Earl Harold,
Since thou hast been with me;
The rust has eaten thy harness bright,
And the rats have eaten thy greyhound light,
That was so fair and free.'

Mary Mother she stooped from heaven;
She wakened Earl Harold out of his sweven,
To don his harness on;
And over the land and over the sea
He wended abroad to his own countrie,
A weary way to gon.

Oh but his beard was white with eld,
Oh but his hair was gray;
He stumbled on by stock and stone,
And as he journeyed he made his moan
Along that weary way.

Earl Harold came to his castle wall;
The gate was burnt with fire;
Roof and rafter were fallen down,
The folk were strangers all in the town,
And strangers all in the shire.

Earl Harold came to a house of nuns,
And he heard the dead-bell toll;
He saw the sexton stand by a grave;
'Now Christ have mercy, who did us save,
Upon yon fair nun's soul.'

The nuns they came from the convent gate
By one, by two, by three;
They sang for the soul of a lady bright
Who died for the love of a traitor knight:
It was his own lady.

He stayed the corpse beside the grave;
'A sign, a sign!' quod he.
'Mary Mother who rulest heaven,
Send me a sign if I be forgiven
By the woman who so loved me.'

A white dove out of the coffin flew;
Earl Harold's mouth it kist;
He fell on his face, wherever he stood;
And the white dove carried his soul to God
Or ever the bearers wist.

The World's Age

Who will say the world is dying?
Who will say our prime is past?
Sparks from Heaven, within us lying,
Flash, and will flash till the last.
Fools! who fancy Christ mistaken;
Man a tool to buy and sell;
Earth a failure, God-forsaken,
Anteroom of Hell.

Still the race of Hero-spirits
Pass the lamp from hand to hand;
Age from age the Words inherits-
'Wife, and Child, and Fatherland.'
Still the youthful hunter gathers
Fiery joy from wold and wood;
He will dare as dared his fathers
Give him cause as good.

While a slave bewails his fetters;
While an orphan pleads in vain;
While an infant lisps his letters,
Heir of all the age's gain;
While a lip grows ripe for kissing;
While a moan from man is wrung;
Know, by every want and blessing,
That the world is young.

The Young Knight: A Parable

A gay young knight in Burley stood,
Beside him pawed his steed so good,
His hands he wrung as he were wood
With waiting for his love O!

'Oh, will she come, or will she stay,
Or will she waste the weary day
With fools who wish her far away,
And hate her for her love O?'

But by there came a mighty boar,
His jowl and tushes red with gore,
And on his curled snout he bore
A bracelet rich and rare O!

The knight he shrieked, he ran, he flew,
He searched the wild wood through and through,
But found nought save a mantle blue,
Low rolled within the brake O!

He twined the wild briar, red and white,
Upon his head the garland dight,
The green leaves withered black as night,
And burnt into his brain O!

A fire blazed up within his breast,
He mounted on an aimless quest,
He laid his virgin lance in rest,
And through the forest drove O!

By Rhinefield and by Osmondsleigh,
Through leat and furze brake fast drove he,
Until he saw the homeless sea,
That called with all its waves O!

He laughed aloud to hear the roar,
And rushed his horse adown the shore,
The deep surge rolled him o'er and o'er,
And swept him down the tide O!

To G.A.G.
A hasty jest I once let fall-
As jests are wont to be, untrue-
As if the sum of joy to you
Were hunt and picnic, rout and ball.

Your eyes met mine: I did not blame;
You saw it: but I touched too near
Some noble nerve; a silent tear
Spoke soft reproach, and lofty shame.

I do not wish those words unsaid.
Unspoilt by praise and pleasure, you
In that one look to woman grew,
While with a child, I thought, I played.

Next to mine own beloved so long!
I have not spent my heart in vain.
I watched the blade; I see the grain;
A woman's soul, most soft, yet strong.

To Miss Mitford: Authoress of
The single eye, the daughter of the light;
Well pleased to recognise in lowliest shade
Some glimmer of its parent beam, and made

By daily draughts of brightness, inly bright.
The taste severe, yet graceful, trained aright
In classic depth and clearness, and repaid
By thanks and honour from the wise and staid-
By pleasant skill to blame, and yet delight,
And high communion with the eloquent throng
Of those who purified our speech and song-
All these are yours. The same examples lure,
You in each woodland, me on breezy moor-
With kindred aim the same sweet path along,
To knit in loving knowledge rich and poor.

Trehill Well
There stood a low and ivied roof,
As gazing rustics tell,
In times of chivalry and song
'Yclept the holy well.

Above the ivies' branchlets gray
In glistening clusters shone;
While round the base the grass-blades bright
And spiry foxglove sprung.

The brambles clung in graceful bands,
Chequering the old gray stone
With shining leaflets, whose bright face
In autumn's tinting shone.

Around the fountain's eastern base
A babbling brooklet sped,
With sleepy murmur purling soft
Adown its gravelly bed.

Within the cell the filmy ferns
To woo the clear wave bent;
And cushioned mosses to the stone
Their quaint embroidery lent.

The fountain's face lay still as glass-
Save where the streamlet free
Across the basin's gnarled lip
Flowed ever silently.

Above the well a little nook
Once held, as rustics tell,
All garland-decked, an image of
The Lady of the Well.

They tell of tales of mystery,
Of darkling deeds of woe;
But no! such doings might not brook

The holy streamlet's flow.

Oh tell me not of bitter thoughts,
Of melancholy dreams,
By that fair fount whose sunny wall
Basks in the western beams.

When last I saw that little stream,
A form of light there stood,
That seemed like a precious gem,
Beneath that archway rude:

And as I gazed with love and awe
Upon that sylph-like thing,
Methought that airy form must be
The fairy of the spring.

Valentine's Day

Oh! I wish I were a tiny browny bird from out the south,
Settled among the alder-holts, and twittering by the stream;
I would put my tiny tail down, and put up my tiny mouth,
And sing my tiny life away in one melodious dream.

I would sing about the blossoms, and the sunshine and the sky,
And the tiny wife I mean to have in such a cosy nest;
And if some one came and shot me dead, why then I could but die,
With my tiny life and tiny song just ended at their best.

Young and Old

When all the world is young, lad,
And all the trees are green;
And every goose a swan, lad,
And every lass a queen;
Then hey for boot and horse, lad,
And round the world away!
Young blood must have its course, lad,
And every dog his day.

When all the world is old, lad,
And all the trees are brown;
And all the sport is stale, lad,
And all the wheels run down;
Creep home, and take your place there,
The spent and maimed among;
God grant you find one face there,
You loved when all was young.

www.ingramcontent.com/pod-product-compliance
Lightning Source LLC
Chambersburg PA
CBHW070108070426
42448CB00038B/2235